Reading Achievement
Comprehension Activities to Promote Essential Reading Skills

Grade 5

by
Jennifer Moore

Table of Contents

Introduction

Welcome to the **Reading Achievement** series! Each book in this series is designed to reinforce the reading skills appropriate for each grade level and to encourage high-level thinking skills. Because reading is an essential part of all disciplines, mastery of these skills can help students succeed in all academic areas. In addition, experiencing success in reading can increase a student's self-esteem and motivate him or her to read more, both in and out of the classroom.

The following reading skills are covered within this book:

- **cause and effect**
- **comprehension**
- **critical thinking**
- **fact or opinion**
- **main ideas/details**
- **sequencing**
- **true or false**
- **vocabulary**

Each **Reading Achievement** book offers challenging questions for students to answer in response to a variety of grade-level appropriate passages. Various types of reading passages are represented in this book, including fiction, nonfiction, poetry, journal entries, charts and graphs, and crossword puzzles. The format and questions are similar to those found on standardized reading tests. The experience students gain from answering questions in this format may help increase their test scores. In addition, these exercises can be used to enhance your school-adopted reading program, to individualize instruction, to provide extra practice for home schoolers, or to review skills between grades.

Each **Reading Achievement** book contains additional features to enhance usability. Four pretests, in standardized test format, have been included at the beginning of each book. The pretests have been designed so that they may be used individually, as four stand-alone tests, or in groups. Another convenient feature is a scoring box on each activity page. This scoring box can be programmed to suit your specific classroom and student needs with total problems, total correct, and score.

Read each passage. Circle the letter beside the correct answer.

Have you ever wanted to help someone paint something like a cabinet with doors, but they told you it was "too hard"? Next time, tell them a secret that will help make the job easier and neater. When you paint a door or a window, you don't want to get paint on the hinges or other metal parts. Sometimes painters put masking tape or painter's tape over them, but here is another tip. First, remove all the metal parts that you can. Then, put a coat of petroleum jelly on all the metal parts you cannot remove. Then, go ahead and paint. When you are finished and the paint has dried, wipe off the petroleum jelly. Any paint that you got on the coated metal parts will come right off!

1. These directions tell you how to:
    A. paint the walls
    C. clean up spilled paint
    B. protect metal parts when you paint
    D. become a painter

2. What do the directions say to do first?
    A. Remove all the metal parts you can.
    C. Wipe up the smeared paint.
    B. Put tape on the metal parts.
    D. Put petroleum jelly on the metal parts.

3. After you remove the metal parts, what should you do next?
    A. Paint the door or window.
    C. Tell someone a secret.
    B. Let the paint dry completely.
    D. Put petroleum on the unremovable metal parts.

4. When the paint has dried and you wipe off the petroleum jelly, you also wipe off:
    A. paint
    C. rust
    B. dirt
    D. painter's tape

One hot humid summer night, a Canadian woman moved her mattress from the bedroom of her house to her porch, hoping it would be cooler out there. She received quite a shock when she woke up the next morning. A large skunk, who apparently also found it too hot to sleep, had curled up right beside her and spent the night. When she saw him, she screamed and jumped up out of the bed. The startled skunk ran off into the woods. Before leaving, however, he left his **calling card.** No longer was it just hot and humid!

5. Why did the lady move her mattress onto her porch?
    A. Her husband was snoring.
    C. to see the stars
    B. It was cooler there.
    D. to pretend she was camping

6. What does **calling card** mean in this story?
    A. a small, printed card
    C. the skunk's scent
    B. a picture
    D. fur

7. The last sentence in the story says "No longer was it just hot and humid!" This means:
    A. that now it was raining
    C. that now the wind was blowing
    B. that now it was smelly
    D. the lady had a skunk to get rid of

4

| Total Problems: | Total Correct: | Score: |

Read each passage. Circle the letter beside the correct answer.

Many people automatically associate motorcycles with reckless young people. But those folks haven't heard about the "Old Timers' Motorcycle Club," where the average age is fifty-five. Many of the members are dignified professionals during the week. They meet every Sunday to race their off-road bikes over rough terrain. The courses are chosen and scouted by a race committee. For safety, participants are required to wear helmets, thick pants, and boots. This also helps members to be recognized as part of the group. There are over two hundred members in the California chapter, which was the first one formed. There are also **chapters** in Oregon, Washington, Canada, and England. Soon there may be international contests. Apparently, on motorcycles, age does not matter—skill does.

1. The main idea of this story is that:
    A. Motorcycle uniforms are important.   B. Motorcycles are reckless.
    C. Not all motorcyclists are young.   D. Riding a motorcycle is dignified.

2. The word **chapters** in this story means:
    A. parts of a book   B. parts of a motorcycle
    C. clubs   D. old-timers

3. Which statement expresses an opinion?
    A. Apparently, on motorcycles, age does not matter—skill does.
    B. Many of the members are dignified professionals during the week.
    C. Soon, there may be international contests.
    D. They meet every Sunday to race their off-road bikes over rough terrain.

4. There are chapters in all these areas, except:
    A. Washington   B. Canada
    C. Oregon   D. Colorado

5. From the story, what can you conclude about members of the "Old Timers' Club"?
    A. All motorcyclists are young.   B. They want to be motorcycle racers.
    C. This is a fun hobby for some.   D. They don't like driving cars.

Five runners entered the 100 meter dash. The runner wearing the number three finished first, with a time of twelve seconds flat. The runner wearing the number two finished fourth. The last runner to finish was wearing the number four. His time was 17.1 seconds.

6. Which conclusion is correct?
    A. The 100 meter dash cannot be run in less than twelve seconds.
    B. If you want to finish first, be sure to have a low number.
    C. All the runners finished in less than 18 seconds.
    D. The other runners did not finish.

Total Problems:	Total Correct:	Score:

Read the passage. Circle the letter beside the correct answer.

There was once a scientist who loved making new kinds of candy. His name was Leo Hirschfield. One day, he made a **novel** chocolate candy shaped like a roll. As he was finishing, he thought of his daughter, Tootsie. You guessed it! Leo Hirschfield had invented the Tootsie Roll®. But he wasn't through coming up with new ideas. At that time, candy was not wrapped, so Leo decided to wrap each Tootsie Roll® individually, and sell them for one cent each. Today, Tootsie Rolls® are still wrapped in paper, and they are still delicious, but unfortunately they do not still cost one cent.

1. The man who invented Tootsie Roll® candy was a:
   A. baker   B. teacher   C. scientist   D. doctor

2. The word **novel** in this story means:
   A. poisonous   B. delicious   C. hard   D. new

3. Tootsie Rolls® were the first candy to be:
   A. sold for one cent   B. named after someone's daughter
   C. eaten   D. wrapped individually

4. The best title for this story is:
   A. Wrapping Candy   B. The Invention of the Tootsie Roll®
   C. Yummy Candy   D. New Kinds of Candy

The chart shows standings for several baseball teams. Refer to the chart to answer the questions.

Team	W	L	R10	Home	Key
Atlanta	71	45	5-5	37-17	W = wins
New York	68	47	8-2	39-18	L = losses
Florida	58	58	7-3	32-30	R10 = record in the last 10 games
Montreal	51	61	4-6	29-29	Home = home wins and losses
Philadelphia	50	65	4-6	26-30	

5. Which team has the best record at home?
   A. Philadelphia   B. Florida   C. Atlanta   D. New York

6. Which team has the worst overall record of wins and losses?
   A. Atlanta   B. Montreal   C. Florida   D. Philadelphia

7. Which team has won the same number of games that it has lost?
   A. New York   B. Florida   C. Montreal   D. Atlanta

8. Which team has the best record for its last ten games?
   A. Florida   B. Atlanta   C. Montreal   D. New York

Total Problems: _____   Total Correct: _____   Score: _____

The chart shows theaters and times for popular movies. Refer to the chart to answer the questions.

Movies Galore	CineMovie	XYZ Theatres
Frenchie and the Fox 2:15, 5:15 *Soccer City* 1:45, 4:15, 7:00, 9:00 *Buffalo Hunter* 1:15, 3:30, 5:30, 7:30, 9:30 *Willow River* 1:30, 3:45, 5:45, 7:45, 9:45	*Soccer City* 1:30, 4:45, 7:15, 9:30 *Buffalo Hunter* 1:30 *Frenchie and the Fox* 1:30 *Willow River* 1:30, 3:00	*Soccer City* 12:30, 2:45, 5:00, 7:30 *Buffalo Hunter* 12:15

1. Which theater has more times and movies from which to choose?
   - A.   Movies Galore
   - B.   CineMovie
   - C.   XYZ Theatres

2. Which movie is showing most often at all the theaters?
   - A. *Frenchie and the Fox*
   - B. *Soccer City*
   - C. *Willow River*
   - D. *Buffalo Hunter*

3. Molly wants to see *Willow River* after school gets out at 3:30. At which theater will she have to see the movie?
   - A.   Movies Galore
   - B.   CineMovie
   - C.   XYZ Theatres

4. What is the latest movie scheduled at any of the theaters?
   - A.   *Frenchie and the Fox*
   - B.   *Soccer City*
   - C.   *Willow River*
   - D.   *Buffalo Hunter*

5. Mrs. Martin has three children, who all want to see a different movie, but she says they all have to go at the same time and to the same theater. At which theater could they do this?
   - A.   Movies Galore
   - B.   CineMovie
   - C.   XYZ Theatres

6. If Mrs. Martin's three children all go to different movies at the same time at the same theater, what time will that be?
   - A.   5:30
   - B.   9:00
   - C.   1:30
   - D.   12:30

7. Jamie wants to see *Soccer City* on Saturday before her soccer game at 2:30. Which feature should she plan to see?
   - A.   Movies Galore at 1:45
   - B.   CineMovie at 1:30
   - C.   XYZ Theatres at 12:30

8. How many possible times are there to see *Buffalo Hunter*?
   - A.   5
   - B.   6
   - C.   7
   - D.   8

9. What is the earliest possible time to see *Soccer City*? _____

Panel 1 (page 4)

Name _____ **Pretest**

Read each passage. Circle the letter beside the correct answer.

Have you ever wanted to help someone paint something like a cabinet with doors, but they told you it was "too hard." Next time, tell them a secret that will help make the job easier and neater. When you paint a door or a window, you don't want to get paint on the hinges or other metal parts. Sometimes painters put masking tape or painter's tape over them, but here is another tip. First, remove all the metal parts that you can. Then, put a coat of petroleum jelly on all the metal parts you cannot remove. Then, go ahead and paint. When you are finished and the paint has dried, wipe off the petroleum jelly. Any paint that you got on the coated metal parts will come right off!

1. These directions tell you how to:
   A. paint the walls (B) protect metal parts when you paint
   C. clean up spilled paint D. become a painter

2. What do the directions say to do first?
   (A) Remove all the metal parts you can. B. Put tape on the metal parts.
   C. Wipe up the smeared paint. D. Put petroleum jelly on the metal parts.

3. After you remove the metal parts, what should you do next?
   A. Paint the door or window. B. Let the paint dry completely.
   C. Tell someone a secret. (D) Put petroleum on the unremovable metal parts.

4. When the paint has dried and you wipe off the petroleum jelly, you also wipe off:
   (A) paint B. dirt
   C. rust D. painter's tape

One hot humid summer night, a Canadian woman moved her mattress from the bedroom of her house to her porch, hoping it would be cooler out there. She received quite a shock when she woke up the next morning. A large skunk, who apparently also found it too hot to sleep, had curled up right beside her and spent the night. When she saw him, she screamed and jumped up out of the bed. The startled skunk ran off into the woods. Before leaving, however, he left his **calling card.** No longer was it just hot and humid!

5. Why did the lady move her mattress onto her porch?
   A. Her husband was snoring. (B) It was cooler there.
   C. to see the stars D. to pretend she was camping

6. What does **calling card** mean in this story?
   A. a small, printed card B. a picture
   (C) the skunk's scent D. fur

7. The last sentence in the story says "No longer was it just hot and humid!" This means:
   A. that now it was raining (B) that now it was smelly
   C. that now the wind was blowing D. the lady had a skunk to get rid of

(4) | Total Problems: | Total Correct: | Score: | © Carson-Dellosa CD-2204

Panel 2 (page 5)

Name _____ **Pretest**

Read each passage. Circle the letter beside the correct answer.

Many people automatically associate motorcycles with reckless young people. But those folks haven't heard about the "Old Timers' Motorcycle Club," where the average age is fifty-five. Many of the members are dignified professionals during the week. They meet every Sunday to race their off-road bikes over rough terrain. The courses are chosen and scouted by a race committee. For safety, participants are required to wear helmets, thick pants, and boots. This also helps members to be recognized as part of the group. There are over two hundred members in the California chapter, which was the first one formed. There are also **chapters** in Oregon, Washington, Canada, and England. Soon there may be international contests. Apparently, on motorcycles, age does not matter—skill does.

1. The main idea of this story is that:
   A. Motorcycle uniforms are important. B. Motorcycles are reckless.
   (C) Not all motorcyclists are young. D. Riding a motorcycle is dignified.

2. The word **chapters** in this story means:
   A. parts of a book B. parts of a motorcycle
   (C) clubs D. old-timers

3. Which statement expresses an opinion?
   (A) Apparently, on motorcycles, age does not matter—skill does.
   B. Many of the members are dignified professionals during the week.
   C. Soon, there may be international contests.
   D. They meet every Sunday to race their off-road bikes over rough terrain.

4. There are chapters in all these areas, except:
   A. Washington B. Canada
   C. Oregon (D) Colorado

5. From the story, what can you conclude about members of the "Old Timers' Club"?
   A. All motorcyclists are young. B. They want to be motorcycle racers.
   (C) This is a fun hobby for some. D. They don't like driving cars.

Five runners entered the 100 meter dash. The runner wearing the number three finished first, with a time of twelve seconds flat. The runner wearing the number two finished fourth. The last runner to finish was wearing the number four. His time was 17.1 seconds.

6. Which conclusion is correct?
   A. The 100 meter dash cannot be run in less than twelve seconds.
   B. If you want to finish first, be sure to have a low number.
   (C) All the runners finished in less than 18 seconds.
   D. The other runners did not finish.

© Carson-Dellosa CD-2204 | Total Problems: | Total Correct: | Score: | (5)

Panel 3 (page 6)

Name _____ **Pretest**

Read the passage. Circle the letter beside the correct answer.

There was once a scientist who loved making new kinds of candy. His name was Leo Hirschfield. One day, he made a **novel** chocolate candy shaped like a roll. As he was finishing, he thought of his daughter, Tootsie. You guessed it! Leo Hirschfield had invented the Tootsie Roll®. But he wasn't through coming up with new ideas. At that time, candy was not wrapped, so Leo decided to wrap each Tootsie Roll® individually, and sell them for one cent each. Today, Tootsie Rolls® are still wrapped in paper, and they are still delicious, but unfortunately they do not still cost one cent.

1. The man who invented Tootsie Roll candy was a:
   A. baker B. teacher (C) scientist D. doctor

2. The phrase **novel** in this story means:
   A. poisonous B. delicious C. hard (D) new

3. Tootsie Rolls were the first candy to be:
   A. sold for one cent B. named after someone's daughter
   C. eaten (D) wrapped individually

4. The best title for this story is:
   A. Wrapping Candy (B) The Invention of the Tootsie Roll
   C. Yummy Candy D. New Kinds of Candy

The chart shows standings for several baseball teams. Refer to the chart to answer the questions.

Team	W	L	R10	Home	Key
Atlanta	71	45	5-5	37-17	W = wins
New York	68	47	8-2	39-18	L = losses
Florida	58	58	7-3	32-30	R10 = record in the last 10 games
Montreal	51	61	4-6	29-29	Home = home wins and losses
Philadelphia	50	65	4-6	26-30	

5. Which team has the best record at home?
   A. Philadelphia B. Florida C. Atlanta (D) New York

6. Which team has the worst overall record of wins and losses?
   A. Atlanta B. Montreal C. Florida (D) Philadelphia

7. Which team has won the same number of games that it has lost?
   A. New York (B) Florida C. Montreal D. Atlanta

8. Which team has the best record for its last ten games?
   A. Florida B. Atlanta C. Montreal (D) New York

(6) | Total Problems: | Total Correct: | Score: | © Carson-Dellosa CD-2204

Panel 4 (page 7)

Name _____ **Pretest**

The chart shows theaters and times for popular movies. Refer to the chart to answer the questions.

Movies Galore	CineMovie	XYZ Theatres
Frenchie and the Fox 2:15, 5:15	*Soccer City* 1:30, 4:45, 7:15, 9:30	*Soccer City* 12:30, 2:45, 5:00, 7:30
Soccer City 1:45, 4:15, 7:00, 9:00	*Buffalo Hunter* 1:30	*Buffalo Hunter* 12:15
Buffalo Hunter 1:15, 3:30, 5:30, 7:30, 9:30	*Frenchie and the Fox* 1:30	
Willow River 1:30, 3:45, 5:45, 7:45, 9:45	*Willow River* 1:30, 3:00	

1. Which theater has more times and movies from which to choose?
   (A) Movies Galore B. CineMovie C. XYZ Theatres

2. Which movie is showing most often at all the theaters?
   A. *Frenchie and the Fox* (B) *Soccer City*
   C. *Willow River* D. *Buffalo Hunter*

3. Molly wants to see *Willow River* after school gets out at 3:30. At which theater will she have to see the movie?
   (A) Movies Galore B. CineMovie C. XYZ Theatres

4. What is the latest movie scheduled at any of the theaters?
   A. *Frenchie and the Fox* B. *Soccer City*
   (C) *Willow River* D. *Buffalo Hunter*

5. Mrs. Martin has three children, who all want to see a different movie, but she says they all have to go at the same time and to the same theater. At which theater could they do this?
   A. Movies Galore (B) CineMovie C. XYZ Theatres

6. If Mrs. Martin's three children all go to different movies at the same time at the same theater, what time will that be?
   A. 5:30 B. 4:30 (C) 1:30 D. 12:30

7. Jamie wants to see *Soccer City* on Saturday before her soccer game at 2:30. Which feature should she plan to see?
   A. Movies Galore at 1:45 B. CineMovie at 1:30 (C) XYZ Theatres at 12:30

8. How many possible times are there to see *Buffalo Hunter*?
   A. 5 B. 6 (C) 7 D. 8

9. What is the earliest possible time to see *Soccer City*? __12:30__

© Carson-Dellosa CD-2204 | Total Problems: | Total Correct: | Score: | (7)

Name _____

Use the information in the chart to answer the following questions.

Chart of Animal Colors for Class Play

Red	Blue	Green	Yellow
Bird	Fish	Frog	Bird
Fish	Bird	Bird	Fish
Dog	Dolphin	Lizard	Dog
Guinea Pig	Butterfly	Worm	Monkey

1. According to the chart, what are the possible colors for the fish? _____

2. Which animals can be green in the play? _____

3. Which animal can be any of the colors? _____

4. In the red group, which animals cannot fly? _____

5. How many different colors can the fish be? _____

6. How many colors can a dog be in the play? _____

7. Which animal can only be yellow? _____

8. How many different animals are there in all? _____

Total Problems:	Total Correct:	Score:

Name _____

Use the information in the table to answer the following questions.

Camp Activities

Monday	Tuesday	Wednesday	Thursday	Friday
(a.m.)	(a.m.)	(a.m.)	(a.m.)	(a.m.)
Crafts	Soccer	Hiking	Tennis	Rafting
Swimming	Swimming	Movies	Cooking	Movies
(p.m.)	(p.m.)	(p.m.)	(p.m.)	(p.m.)
Horseback riding	Tennis	Book club	Woodworking	Skating
Volleyball	Relay races	Aerobics	Swimming	Dancing
Beach trips	Shopping	Crafts	Shopping	Swimming
Biking	Cooking	Swimming	Rock climbing	Free time

1. What day(s) is soccer an option for the campers? _____

2. What sedentary activity is scheduled for Wednesday mornings? _____

3. When is crafts offered in the afternoon? _____

4. What activity is offered every day of the week? _____

5. On what two days is cooking offered? _____

6. What ball sport(s) is/are offered on Monday? _____

7. When is free time offered? _____

8. What activities are offered more than once during the week? _____

   _____

9. When is skating offered? _____

10. Which day(s) has/have the most athletic activities offered? _____

Total Problems:	Total Correct:	Score:

Name _____

Use the information from the graph to answer the following questions.

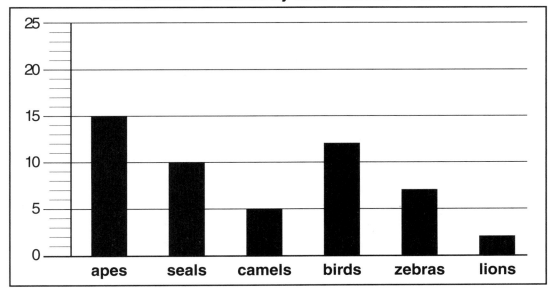

Zoo Animals Counted by Mrs. Sullivan's Class

1. How many seals did the students see? _____

2. How many more apes than camels were seen? _____

3. Which animal was most numerous at the zoo? _____

4. How many zebras were there? _____

5. What animal were there only 2 of at the zoo? _____

6. How many animals in all were seen by the students? _____

7. How many birds were there? _____

8. How many more zebras were seen than camels? _____

| Total Problems: | Total Correct: | Score: |

Read the passage. Determine the sequence of events and number the six statements in the order they occur in the passage.

Juan's Time Line

Juan was assigned a project in school that would require him to make a time line of his life. His teacher told the class to use a large poster to display the time line. The students were to use pictures of themselves to show each year of their lives from birth to present. With each year of their lives, there should also be a corresponding picture and written description of an event in the world.

This project meant Juan had to do some research. Juan took his assignment sheet and got a sheet of poster paper from the closet. He then drew a ten-year time line on the poster.

Next, he gathered research to provide the notable world events. He found some of the information on the Internet. He carefully wrote a description of each event on the poster. Finally, he pasted some pictures of himself and world events on the poster. Now, Juan was finished with his project.

1. _____ Juan wrote a brief description beside each picture.

2. _____ He gathered information on notable events.

3. _____ He pasted pictures of himself and famous events on his poster.

4. _____ He drew a line for the time line that would represent 10 years.

5. _____ Juan got an assignment for a time line from his teacher.

6. _____ Juan got a piece of poster paper.

Total Problems:	Total Correct:	Score:

Read the passage and each question that follows. Circle the letter beside the correct answer. Refer to the passage if necessary.

Learning to Swim

Margaret is an excellent swimmer. Many times people ask her how she became such a good swimmer. She always credits her early training in the water to her current success. Margaret tells people there are a few important steps to follow in learning to swim and appreciating the water, rather than fear it.

First, it is important for the swimmer to relax and put in his feet. Then, he should proceed to standing in shallow areas, wading in further as desired. As the water level reaches the legs, hips, and chest, the swimmer should push the water back and forth to feel the water. The swimmer can go deeper into the water letting the entire body be submerged, except for the head.

Then, standing in shallow water and holding onto something stable, the swimmer should take a deep breath and put his face in the water for a few seconds. After trying this a few times, the swimmer can try blowing out air to create bubbles in the water while his face is in the water.

Once a beginning swimmer has felt the sensation of water on his face and is no longer scared, he can try learning a few strokes. When learning strokes, it is important to practice first with only the hands and feet. Later, the swimmer can put his face in the water and try to move through the water rhythmically.

1. What is the first thing a beginning swimmer should do?
   A.   put in his face
   B.   put in his feet
   C.   learn the proper strokes
   D.   wade into the deep end

2. What is necessary to do right before learning the strokes?
   A.   splash the water with your hands
   B.   stand in the shallow end
   C.   become used to the sensation of water on your face
   D.   learn to dive correctly

3. What is the last step for a beginning swimmer?
   A.   learning to call for the lifeguard
   B.   learning to swim in competition
   C.   learning to care for a drowning person
   D.   learning the strokes and moving the body

Read each passage and question. Circle the letter beside the correct answer.

Gravity

One day Dan and his father were talking about why things fall down when they are dropped. His father explained that the earth has a natural pull called gravity. Gravity pulls things on the Earth's surface toward the center of the Earth. Dan was confused. His father began showing him how objects are drawn or pulled toward the Earth's center. He demonstrated by rolling a ball down a hill. Then he showed Dan the leaves in the yard and reminded him that they just fell that way. The objects try to get to the lowest place possible. None can actually get to the Earth's center because it is covered by many other objects. Gravity is natural to us and we depend on it for many things we do

1. What is the main idea of this story?
    A. Earth
    B. gravity
    C. falling
    D. atmosphere

The Circus

A girl went whirling up into the air and after doing two somersaults landed directly on the feet of the man lying on his back. Jan looked on in awe as the circus people completed one death-defying act after another. The circus amazed Jan. She liked the acrobats, the animals, and especially the happy feeling she got from being at the circus. The costumes were brightly colored and the tricks were dazzling. Going to the circus was exciting because it was different every year and the clowns always made Jan laugh. As Jan left the circus, she promised herself that she would be back again next year.

2. What is the main idea of this story?
    A. Jan likes the circus.
    B. The circus is in town every year.
    C. The acrobats have improved.
    D. The animals are better every year.

Total Problems:	Total Correct:	Score:

Read each passage and question. Circle the letter beside the correct answer.

Clouds

Clouds look like giant balls of cotton, but they are not made of cotton at all. Rather, clouds are formations in the Earth's atmosphere that consist mainly of water. A part of the water cycle, clouds are accumulations of water that have evaporated from the Earth's surface and collected in a large area high above the earth. The evaporated water becomes vapor and expands and cools as it rises into the air. Since air can only hold a certain amount of water, the vapor can change to water again if the air gets cooler. This becomes rain on Earth. If the temperature is cold enough, the water vapor changes to ice rather than to water, thus ice or snow is produced. Clouds can tell us a lot about the temperature, the moisture in the air, and the potential for a storm.

1. What is the main idea of this paragraph?
   A. Clouds are little weather stations.
   B. Clouds usually help in predicting the weather.
   C. how clouds are formed
   D. where clouds usually are in the atmosphere

Learning to Read

Learning to read is something that is usually done in the early grades. Everyone can benefit in many ways from knowing how to read. Putting sounds with letters and then combining letters and sounds to make words is the basic level of learning to read. As the reading process continues, it is imperative to practice all the reading skills. Reading then becomes the main tool for getting information on practically any topic. Being able to read is a huge factor in one's success—both academically and professionally. It enables a person to be knowledgeable in an ever-changing world.

2. The main idea of this paragraph is:
   A. It is tough to learn how to read.
   B. Reading is fundamental to many other things.
   C. Reading can be difficult at times.
   D. Most children can read before they enter kindergarten.

Total Problems:	Total Correct:	Score:

Read the passage and place a check in the blank next to each statement that is a fact from the paragraph.

Abraham Lincoln

Abraham Lincoln was the sixteenth president of the United States of America. He was a lawyer before becoming president and had a reputation for being extremely honest. Many of his political accomplishments include helping other people overcome adversity. These deeds certainly support how dedicated Mr. Lincoln was to the people of his country. Mr. Lincoln is known for his efforts to abolish slavery. He was dissatisfied with the injustices of slavery and was quick to see other people being oppressed or mistreated. The north and south did not agree for many years on the topic of slavery, but after years of civil war, slavery was abolished in the United States.

1. _____ Mr. Lincoln was known as an honest man.

2. _____ The ending of slavery is not considered an accomplishment of Lincoln's.

3. _____ Mr. Lincoln was the sixteenth president of the United States.

4. _____ Before becoming president, Mr. Lincoln did not have a career.

5. _____ Mr. Lincoln was committed to helping people in hardships.

Total Problems:	Total Correct:	Score:

Read the passage and place a check in the blank next to each statement that is a fact from the paragraph.

Learning from Playing

Children learn from playing. It may sound strange, but it is true. Playing with toys can help babies learn about their environment. They can also learn that they are doing things themselves that cause certain events to happen. They begin to notice that a toy moves if they push it, a button may squeak if pressed, and a ball rolls when nudged. Learning to do new things is often a bridge of experience the child has had with an earlier situation. Remembering one event and relating it to another is an elaborate form of learning called reasoning.

Helping children play with a variety of toys is a wonderful way to foster early learning. It is important, however, to remember that all objects are not toys. Parents and child care workers should be very careful when selecting toys to give young children.

1. _____ Children can learn from playing with toys.

2. _____ All toys either squeak or roll.

3. _____ A toy is any object that is fun to hold.

4. _____ Children, at a relatively early age, understand they can do things to objects.

5. _____ Parents should make careful toy purchases for their children.

6. _____ Reasoning is when an old experience is related to a newer one.

7. _____ Usually, small children do not enjoy playing with balls or stuffed animals.

Total Problems:	Total Correct:	Score:

17

Read each passage and question. Circle the letter beside the correct answer.

Paul and Wade

Paul and Wade are best friends. Paul is very messy and Wade is very neat and organized. Many times Wade has offered to help Paul become better organized. One day Paul misplaced a very important letter. It was his birthday letter from his grandmother. It had a twenty-dollar bill inside, too. He was very upset about losing the letter and he went to Wade to tell him that it was time to turn over a new leaf. He asked Wade for some help in getting everything in his bedroom organized. The two boys got busy with their work and after a few hours the room looked great. Paul even found the missing letter underneath a stack of papers on his desk.

1. What is meant in the paragraph by the phrase, "turn over a new leaf"?
    A. He should do more yard work each day for his father.
    B. He should make a change for the better.
    C. He should plant trees so there will be more leaves in the environment.
    D. He should try something new whenever possible.

The Birdhouse

Donna and Mary had been working on their masterpiece birdhouse for the Garden Club show. They were getting very frustrated with the wire base they had created. It did not seem to be strong enough to hold the sides of the house up. There must be some way to make a base strong enough to support the rest of the structure. Donna had made a large frame with plenty of room inside for the birds. She had also measured the sections accurately and had just enough material to cover the entire birdhouse. After some discussion, Mary and Donna decided that not all of their design was bad. It was just necessary to remake the base. There was no need to throw the baby out with the bath water. A few changes would make the birdhouse into just what they designed. Donna went inside to find her father for help. He could make a wooden base. Mr. Johnson gladly came to help the girls and soon they were on their way to a splendid birdhouse for the show.

2. What is meant by the phrase "no need to throw the baby out with the bath water"?
    A. Just because one part of a big project is not good, does not mean the entire thing is bad.
    B. Everyone has had a bad day before and if one thing goes wrong, that is not too bad.
    C. Everyone should be more patient when bathing children so that they are not accidentally hurt.
    D. Most people like to work on a project for a long time and get through their mistakes.

Total Problems:	Total Correct:	Score:

Read each passage and question. Circle the letter beside the correct answer.

Shawn and Jason's Fort

Shawn liked to go exploring in the woods behind his house. On Saturday, his friend Jason came over to play with him. The two boys decided to go to the woodsy area and look for fallen tree limbs and things to use for a fort. They had been planning all winter to build a fort when the weather warmed up. Shawn knew exactly where to begin looking and the two boys were on their mission. Jason soon found a large tree limb and tried to pull it up from underneath some other brush. He pulled and pulled but never was able to make it budge. He yelled for Shawn to come help him. Shawn came over and Jason told him that the tree limb would be great, but it must weigh a ton. The two boys pulled and pulled but never succeeded in getting the limb.

1. What is meant by the phrase "it must weigh a ton"?
    A.   An object is over 2,000 pounds according to standard measurement.
    B.   The object is extremely heavy.
    C.   Sometimes trees get heavier as they become older and their branches fall.
    D.   Every tree is extremely heavy.

Beth and Meg's Brownies

Beth and Meg were in the kitchen making their famous brownies. Well, at least they thought they were famous. The girls were best friends and they loved doing things together, especially cooking. They had been in the kitchen for only a few minutes when Meg accidentally dropped the entire bowl of brownie mix. It landed on the floor with a thud. The girls looked at the mess in total disbelief. Their day of brownie making was ruined. Beth's mother heard the noise and came into the kitchen to see what was going on. The girls looked so disappointed and quietly explained the accident. Beth's mother smiled and said that before they knew it gray skies would clear up. She helped the girls clean up the mess and then began a second batch of brownies.

2. What did Beth's mother mean by "gray skies would clear up"?
    A.   When making a recipe there should not be more than two people helping.
    B.   Sometimes, if too many people help do a job, it is not very helpful.
    C.   Usually, people need help only if they ask someone for it.
    D.   Bad events will soon pass and good things will come.

Total Problems:	Total Correct:	Score:

19

Read each passage and question. Circle the letter beside the correct answer.

Taylor's Afternoon at Mom's Office

Every Wednesday Taylor liked going to her mother's office after school. Soon after Taylor arrived, there would be about ten cars arriving with dogs inside. Taylor would watch each owner park his or her car, get out and open the door for his or her precious pooch. All the dogs and the owners would gather in a clear area of the parking lot, in a circle. Soon, a lady would arrive and walk to the center of the circle. After giving a few directions, the crowd of dogs and people would begin to walk in an orderly fashion around and around the circle. Taylor loved watching this and she would beg her mother to wait a few more minutes before leaving so she could see the dogs a little longer.

1. Most likely, what is the scene Taylor is watching?
    A. A pet store is taking all of the dogs out for a chance to exercise.
    B. A dog obedience class is starting.
    C. It is a pet adoption day at a nearby animal hospital.
    D. The local police station is training dogs to help in police work.

Mark and Amy

Mark and Amy entered the building and quickly got in line to buy their tickets. After they each had a ticket, they passed through another door, giving the man at the door their tickets. He tore the tickets in half and returned a stub to them to keep. Mark saw a few friends he recognized and went over to speak while Amy got in line for popcorn and sodas. Soon the two friends walked down a carpeted hallway and entered a large, dark room. They selected two seats near the back of the room and began munching on their snacks. Soon the screen before them lit up, and loud music began to play.

2. Most likely, where are Mark and Amy?
    A. at a movie theater
    B. at a restaurant
    C. at a shopping mall
    D. at a football game

Total Problems: _____   Total Correct: _____   Score: _____

Read each passage and question. Circle the letter beside the correct answer.

Nancy and Sonya

Nancy and Sonya were so nervous about their performances. They only had to wait now. What were the judges going to decide? The girls were giddy with anxious anticipation. Nancy and Sonya knew they had practiced and had memorized all the cheers perfectly. Certainly they would make the squad. They had been taking gymnastics for seven years! Their jumps and flips were almost perfect. The girls felt like the time was just crawling by. Hopefully the results would be good and the girls would have another dream come true! They were so excited about possibly being on the sidelines of the football games next season!

1. Most likely, what were the girls doing?
    A.   taking lessons on how to be cheerleaders
    B.   trying out for the cheerleading squad
    C.   trying to be on the school gymnastic team
    D.   trying to see who had a better jump than the other one

Lee and Dad

Lee and his dad were packing their things in the car. They had a cooler with plenty of drinks and snacks. They also had on their baseball caps. Once the sports-crazy-duo drove away, they began chatting about the plans for the day. Lee asked his father several times about the tickets and his father assured him they were in his pocket. In minutes, the stadium was in sight. Lee could hardly stay calm. He grabbed a few drinks and snacks from the cooler and stuffed them into his backpack. They parked the car and headed for the huge black gates. Once inside, Lee noticed a sign that pointed to an area where kids could run the bases before the game. Mr. Wilson agreed to let his son participate while he watched. Lee soon came back to his dad and the two headed off to find their seats for the day.

2. Most likely, what are Lee and his father doing?
    A.   going to baseball practice
    B.   going to the batting cages
    C.   going to a baseball game
    D.   going to baseball summer camp

| Total Problems: | Total Correct: | Score: | **21** |

Read the journal entries and answer the questions on the following page.

Monday, December 7

Sara told Jenny today that she was going to start taking ice-skating lessons. I started taking lessons only a week ago and now my whole fifth-grade class is going to copy me! I think there are other things people could do for fun and exercise. Oh well, Mom says it is flattering when others do things like you. I don't see that. I like ice-skating because that is something I can do without my little brother! I know Mom needs a lot of help with him, but he really can take up a lot of my time.

Tuesday, December 8

I hope I did okay on my science test today! That class really can be hard sometimes. I really like Mrs. Johnson for a teacher. She explains things really well. Plus the experiments she lets us do are so much fun. Surely, I made an "A" on that test. I hope so, anyway!

Wednesday, December 9

My dad returns from his business trip on Thursday. I can't wait. He promised to pick me up from school and take me to get an ice cream, a new pair of jeans, and a necklace. Shopping with Dad is a lot of fun. I think it is because he doesn't really remember what I already have at home. So, we don't fuss about clothes like Mom and I do.

Thursday, December 10

Wow, I cannot believe it is already about to be Christmas! This year has gone by so quickly! I hope we get to go to my grandmother's this year for Christmas. She is retired and has all this time to do stuff for my little brother and me. She is a great cook! She makes great cookies and cakes, and her turkey and stuffing are fantastic!

Read each question and circle the letter beside the correct answer.

1. Monica's father would be returning soon from:
    A.   a ball game
    B.   work
    C.   a business trip
    D.   a movie

2. What grade is Monica in at school?
    A.   4th
    B.   3rd
    C.   5th
    D.   6th

3. Why does Monica feel that Sara and Jenny are "copying" her?
    A.   They wear the same kinds of clothes as Monica.
    B.   They are beginning to take ice-skating lessons.
    C.   They are in her class and watch her all of the time.
    D.   They are trying to talk like her.

4. What does Monica like about her science teacher?
    A.   She likes the tests because they are usually hard.
    B.   She likes it when the teacher lets the class go outside.
    C.   She likes the experiments and the way she explains things.
    D.   She likes the cool clothes her teacher wears to class.

5. What does Monica like about visiting her grandmother?
    A.   She likes to play with her dog and cats.
    B.   She likes to help her grandmother work in the flower beds.
    C.   She likes when her grandmother tells funny stories to her.
    D.   She likes her grandmother's cooking.

6. With whom does Monica enjoy shopping?
    A.   her dad
    B.   her mom
    C.   Jenny
    D.   Sara

Total Problems:	Total Correct:	Score:

Read the journal entries and answer the questions on the following page.

<u>Tuesday, November 5</u>

I don't know why, but for some reason I have decided to start writing a journal. My teacher said that it can be a fun thing to do. She even said that people just write about their thoughts in a journal so it doesn't have to be fancy or for anyone else to read. I like that. I think I'll do this for a few weeks to see how it goes.

<u>Wednesday, November 6</u>

Well, today is day two of my journal. I had a pretty good day at school. I think my friend Brent is crazy though. He said he liked our substitute teacher in math today. We usually have Mrs. Anderson and today she was sick so we had a sub. Her name was Mrs. Jenkins. I thought she looked funny, but Brent said she explained division to him very well. I prefer waiting to talk to Mrs. Anderson when she gets back. Well, that's all I can write today. I have to go to football practice now.

<u>Thursday, November 7</u>

I am so tired today! I think our coach expects us to be like professional football players or something. We had a hard practice yesterday. We certainly should win our game tomorrow afternoon. Well, I have to do my homework now. I'll write more tomorrow.

<u>Friday, November 8</u>

I have really surprised myself about writing in my journal. I even think about it at school and I plan some things to write when I get home. Like today, I had a great time at football practice and my friend José is going to come over to my house on Saturday. I like hanging around with him. I don't think I will tell him about my journal though, since it's kind of private. I don't want to tell anyone really. Maybe I will tell my mom, but that's all. And speaking of Mom, I hear her calling for me. Until tomorrow!

Read each question and circle the letter beside the correct answer.

1. Who is the writer's friend?
   A. Brent
   B. Scott
   C. Mrs. Anderson
   D. Mrs. Jenkins

2. What event takes place for Scott on Wednesday?
   A. football practice
   B. a parade
   C. a football game
   D. a birthday party

3. What does Brent like about Mrs. Jenkins?
   A. She's a good artist.
   B. She likes football.
   C. She explains division well.
   D. She tells funny jokes

4. When is Scott's game?
   A. Tuesday
   B. Wednesday
   C. Thursday
   D. Friday

5. What caused Scott to stop writing in his journal on Friday?
   A. His friend Jose came over to his house.
   B. His mom was calling for him.
   C. His sister came into his room.
   D. He was tired of keeping a journal.

Total Problems: _____ Total Correct: _____ Score: _____

Read the poem and each question that follows. Circle the letter beside the correct answer.

A Lady

A lady wore a hat to the town's parade.
It had a big, red flower perched on top.
I saw her somewhere later, drinking lemonade;
I guess she prefers that drink to plain old soda pop.

She did look peculiar in her flower hat;
I'd never, ever seen anything like that before.
She also had a bag in which she carried her cat.
But, I heard she's really nice, and knows my best friend Matt!

Then, just two days later I saw her wear a sock.
I think it was pink and orange with big red polka dots.
She looked a little funny, but it wasn't quite a shock,
'Cause it seems she just likes dressing and visiting town a lot.

1. What is the meaning of the poem?
   A. A lady is trying to dress for going downtown.
   B. A bystander notices a lady who is unusual.
   C. A parade usually has a variety of people.
   D. A town has different people who like different things.

2. When did the author first notice the lady?
   A. at the restaurant
   C. at a store
   B. at the parade
   D. at a party

3. What was the lady wearing on her hat?
   A. a blue butterfly
   C. a red flower
   B. a purple dot
   D. a button

4. What was the lady carrying in her bag?
   A. a cat
   C. a bird
   B. a sandwich
   D. a dog

5. What had polka dots?
   A. the lady's sock
   C. a bird's cage
   B. the lady's bag
   D. a box

Total Problems: Total Correct: Score:

Read the poem and each question that follows. Circle the letter beside the correct answer.

My Rainbow

I wished for a rainbow to span through the sky.
Bystanders would notice as it catches the eye.

The colors to be vivid and easy to see,
I'd walk through the city with it following me.

Tall buildings may stretch to amazing heights,
But leave my rainbow in perfect sight.

I'd really be lucky to have such a treasure,
Which would also bring others moments of pleasure.

My rainbow and me, a wonderful pair,
My wish, my hope, for sometime out there.

1. What was the person in the poem hoping for?
   A. rain   B. sunshine   C. a rainbow   D. tall buildings

2. Where did the person imagine seeing the rainbow?
   A. in a grassy field   B. over a pond
   C. in a desert   D. in a city

3. Why does the person seem to think that the rainbow is following him or her?
   A. Because it continues to be visible in the city among all of the buildings.
   B. Because it is moving through the sky with the force of the wind.
   C. Because he or she is in a car and the rainbow seems to be moving.
   D. Because most rainbows move around in the sky.

4. What human ability did the writer say the buildings seem to have?
   A. lying down   B. stretching   C. running   D. sitting

5. According to the poem, why does the person want a rainbow?
   A. Because he or she doesn't have very many friends.
   B. Because he or she really likes rainbows and feels they bring happiness.
   C. Because he or she has never seen one before.
   D. Because he or she thinks they look funny in the sky.

Total Problems:	Total Correct:	Score:

Read the poem and each question that follows. Circle the letter beside the correct answer.

My Walk

I walked home from school the other day,
And took a different, more scenic, way.

A small red bird was eating some bread.
As he nibbled, I noticed him bobbing his head.

When I walked on further down my new path,
I saw this squirrel giving his tail a bath.

He didn't even notice that I stopped to look,
Nor did the old man who was reading his book.

The park is a neat and wonderful place.
It gives me a smile right on my face.

1. Where was the person when he or she saw the bird?
   A. at school   B. at home
   C. at the park   D. in the city

2. Why did the person go home a different way?
   A. It was a faster way home.
   B. It was a more scenic way.
   C. It was raining and this way was easier.
   D. He or she wanted to meet a friend.

3. Why did the person stop to watch things in the park?
   A. He or she found them interesting.
   B. It was part of a homework assignment.
   C. The old man told him or her to watch those things.
   D. He or she will never see a bird like that again.

4. What does the author mean by the word "bobbing"?
   A. moving from side to side
   B. moving in circles
   C. moving up and down
   D. making very still

| Total Problems: | Total Correct: | Score: |

Read the passage and answer the questions that follow.

One Big Cat

Graceful, alert, and cunning, leopards are the third largest animal of the cat family. They live mostly in Africa and Asia. Only the lion and tiger are larger cats than the leopard. A large male can weigh up to one hundred sixty pounds. A big female may weigh up to eighty pounds.

Leopards are usually light tan with many black spots close together. Leopards are fierce animals who usually eat meat. They hunt their prey and rarely attack humans. These animals are unbelievably strong and can lift other animals very close to their own size. They are excellent climbers and often hide in trees to eat or watch for approaching prey.

While leopards are naturally wild, some have been captured and taught to be somewhat gentle. However, they are never suitable house pets. Their instincts are to hunt and kill their food. They are ferocious animals that belong in the wild.

1. What animals in the cat family are larger than the leopard? _____

   _____

2. Where do leopards often hide to capture their prey? _____

   _____

3. Why are leopards not suitable house pets? _____

   _____

4. On what continents are leopard populations usually found? _____

   _____

5. What do leopards look like? _____

   _____

Total Problems:	Total Correct:	Score:

Name _____

Read the passage and answer the questions that follow.

Scotland

Scotland is one of four countries that make up the United Kingdom of Great Britain and Northern Ireland. Scotland is a constitutional monarchy and Queen Elizabeth II is the head of state. The two largest cities in Scotland are Glasgow and Edinburgh. Edinburgh is the capital although it is smaller than Glasgow.

English is the country's dominant language and people are known for their closely knit families. The Scots refer to their larger family as a clan. Each clan often has a tartan plaid fabric they use to identify themselves. This tartan is commonly made into a formal clothing article called a kilt.

The economy of Scotland is supported by trade and manufacturing. The coastal ports allow ample opportunities for Scotland to import and export goods. Much of Scotland's food is imported while manufactured products are major exports.

Scotland is a beautiful country famous for its mountainous terrain, known as the highlands. Many tourists visit Scotland for its beauty, history, and leisure activities. The game of golf was invented in Scotland in the 1100s and remains popular there today. Other favorite sports of the Scots include association football—or soccer, hiking, mountain climbing, and fishing. The Highland Games take place each year and include events such as track, dance, tossing the caber, bagpipe playing and others.

1. What is the capital of Scotland?_____

2. What term is used by Scottish people that means "family"?_____

3. What sport was invented in Scotland?_____

4. How could the land in Scotland be described?_____

5. Who is the head of state for Scotland?_____

Total Problems: _____ Total Correct: _____ Score: _____

Name _____

Refer to the passage on page 30 to solve this puzzle.

Scotland Crossword Puzzle

Across

    4   the capital of Scotland

    6   another term for "family group"

    7   this popular sport or game was invented in Scotland

    8   often called "football," a popular Scottish sport

Down

    1   a common landform in Scotland

    2   a large city in Scotland

    3   a skirt-like article of clothing

    4   the main language of Scotland

    5   a popular musical instrument in Scotland

Read the passage and answer the questions on the following page.

Robert Browning

Robert Browning was born in May of 1812 in London. His wealthy parents were able to provide lots of books for him to read. His father, a banker, encouraged him to learn all about the arts and literature. He attended school rather irregularly, but did eventually enter college. He did not ever complete his education, instead he began to publish many of his poems. Browning is best known for his romantic monologue poetry. He received some criticism for his first published poem as it took a deep look into very personal things in his life. Browning felt this was too harsh and had a difficult time overcoming the remarks. After that, he wrote in a way that exemplified his ability to seem emotional, but the emotions were not from personal experiences.

Writing was the way Robert Browning found he could communicate his thoughts and feelings. This became reality as he courted the lovely Elizabeth Barrett, who was also a poet. Miss Barrett lived with her father because she was in poor health and unable to live alone. She was able to move only in a wheelchair. She had written to Browning about his poetry that interested her and soon the letter writing turned into a romantic courtship.

Their relationship developed so far that Browning took Elizabeth on a trip and they were secretly married. Elizabeth's doctors felt her health would improve if she moved to Italy. When she married Mr. Browning, he immediately took her to Italy where she received excellent care.

As Mr. Browning's work did not provide him with a large salary, he and his wife lived on a very small income for a long time. One day a cousin of Elizabeth's from London began sending her one hundred pounds a week. Just before he died, he willed her a total of eleven thousand pounds. The couple did not have to worry about money after that. They remained in Italy and visited France and England on vacations. Today many modern poets continue to study the works of Robert Browning. He influenced many with his incredible talent for romantic monologue. This was by far his greatest accomplishment and contribution to poetry. His plays were not as popular as his poetry, yet he did receive recognition for a variety of writings.

Read each question. Circle the letter beside the correct answer.

1. What country is Robert Browning from originally?
   A.   Ireland
   B.   England
   C.   United States
   D.   Italy

2. How did he and Elizabeth Barrett meet each other?
   A.   telephone calls
   B.   at school
   C.   through letters
   D.   in the hospital

3. Where did Elizabeth live when she was writing to Mr. Browning?
   A.   with her father
   B.   with her cousin
   C.   with her sister
   D.   with her neighbor

4. What did Robert and Elizabeth do secretly?
   A.   write poetry
   B.   get married
   C.   move to Italy
   D.   teach her to walk

5. Why did they move to Italy?
   A.   for better health
   B.   for better jobs
   C.   for more money
   D.   to help others

6. How did the couple get money for living expenses?
   A.   They received money from her father and insurance.
   B.   They received money from his writing and hers.
   C.   They were paid for his work and received money from a will.
   D.   They performed plays and taught poetry at local colleges.

7. What is Robert Browning's greatest literary contribution?
   A.   writing poems with a romantic monologue
   B.   writing plays with sad endings
   C.   helping his wife improve her health
   D.   writing letters to people to cheer them up

Total Problems:	Total Correct:	Score:

Name _____

Refer to the passage on page 32 to solve this puzzle.

Robert Browning Crossword Puzzle

Across

  3   the month of Robert Browning's birth

  5   a kind of relative—Elizabeth was sent money from hers

  6   wife of Robert Browning

  8   a way of communicating through the mail

  9   the type of writing Browning is famous for

Down

  1   having to do with one's feelings

  2   place of Mr. Browning's birth

  4   his father's occupation

  7   A doctor suggested Elizabeth move to this country.

Total Problems: _____   Total Correct: _____   Score: _____

Read the passage and answer the questions on the following page.

Sir Edmund Hillary

Sir Edmund Hillary was the first person to climb Mt. Everest in the Himalayas. Mt. Everest stands over twenty-nine thousand feet tall and is five and one half miles above sea level. Sir Edmund completed his climb on May 29, 1953. Since then, there have been many expeditions to reach the summit. Many have had success, but some climbers have fallen victim to the dangers along the way, such as steep slopes, extreme cold, thin air, and avalanches.

Mt. Everest is located north of India in the Himalayan range. Many surveyors and climbers in nearby Tibet and Nepal have been attracted to the mountain's challenging landscape. Climbing the south side of the mountain is most common. Some have attempted to climb the west ridge, which is more difficult. Still today there are exuberant mountain climbers and thrill seeking individuals who will attempt the feat of reaching the summit of the tallest mountain in the world—Mt. Everest.

Name _____

Read each statement and decide if it is true or false. Place a T or F in the blank next to the statement.

1. _____ Sir Edmund Hillary was the first to climb Mt. Everest.

2. _____ Mt. Everest is 5½ miles above sea level.

3. _____ The Himalayas are located north of India.

4. _____ Cold temperatures, strong winds, and steep slopes help climbers reach the top easily.

5. _____ The summit is the highest point of a mountain.

Reader's Response: Write why you think some people enjoy mountain climbing.

_____
_____
_____
_____
_____
_____
_____
_____
_____
_____
_____
_____
_____
_____
_____
_____

Total Problems: **Total Correct:**   **Score:**

Name _____

Refer to the passage on page 35 to solve this puzzle.

Sir Edmund Hillary Crossword Puzzle

Across

5 word often used to describe a mountain climbing trip
6 flexible heavy cord used for tying and pulling
7 a large mass of snow or ice moving swiftly down a mountainside
9 a very straight and high incline

Down

1 the very top of the mountain
2 not straight; an incline
3 a very large hill, great for climbing
4 a high overhanging face of rock
5 the tallest mountain in the world
8 to move up a mountain

Read the passage and answer the questions on the following page.

Critters Called Clams

What has one foot and sprays water at its enemies? Well, it's a clam. You may be fortunate enough one day to actually find a live clam in its shell on the beach. However, the clam notices danger very quickly and will pull its one foot inside its shell and just lie there. You can try as hard as you can to open the shell with your hands, but it won't open. The clam's soft body lives in the shell and it travels on land with the one foot it has. When danger seems to be near, the clam can spray water toward the area of danger. This is its way of protecting itself.

Sea gulls like to eat clams. Many times you may find empty clam shells on the shore. Those clams were probably eaten by a sea gull. Often times the clam can even escape from the sea gull's watchful eye. If a clam senses danger and the predator does not leave after being sprayed with water, the clam can bury itself in the sand and all you may see is a bubble in the sand. This is often hard to see and many times clams remain safe from hunters that way.

Clam digging is the way most fishermen harvest their clams. Just at the edge of the surf on the beach, one can dig up the sand and often find clams hidden. They are attempting to hide until they choose to go back out to sea. In restaurants clams are a popular seafood item and are often served steamed in their shells.

Name _____

Read each question and write your answer in the space provided.

1. How does the clam travel on shore? _____

_____

2. What does the clam do when danger seems near? _____

_____

_____

3. Who enjoys eating clams? _____

_____

4. How can fishermen gather clams? _____

_____

_____

5. What is the clam's body like? _____

_____

6. Where do clams often hide? _____

_____

7. Why are clam shells often found on shore with no clams inside? _____

_____

_____

8. How can someone tell if a clam is hidden in the sand? _____

_____

_____

| Total Problems: | Total Correct: | Score: |

Read the passage and the statements that follow. Decide if each statement is true or false. Place a T or F in the blank next to each statement.

Great Ball of Fire

The sun is over ninety million miles from Earth. Measuring over one hundred times the Earth's diameter, the sun is a huge ball of gasses glowing at the center of the solar system. The sun is the closest star to Earth.

While the size seems to be enormous, it is important to remember that without the sun, human beings could not live. The heat and light provided by the sun sustains life for every plant and animal on earth.

Temperatures on Earth are greatly affected by the sun. When the sun's light hits the Earth at a direct angle, that area experiences a warm or hot season. When the sun's light hits the Earth at an indirect angle, that area experiences a cool or cold season.

Scientists have studied the sun for many years. They have discovered many things about the sun that have helped humanity. They predict the sun will continue to be a source of energy for another five billion years.

1. _____ The sun is a star.

2. _____ The sun sustains life on earth.

3. _____ The sun is in another solar system near us.

4. _____ The angle of sunlight affects temperatures on earth.

5. _____ The sun will no longer exist in five million years.

6. _____ People use the sun for heat and light.

Total Problems:	Total Correct:	Score:

Refer to the passage on page 40 to solve this puzzle.

Great Ball of Fire Crossword Puzzle

Across

  1 The sun is one of these heavenly objects.
  3 The sun is in the center of this (two words).
  4 The sun provides this to keep us warm.
  5 opposite of dark

Down

  1 professionals who study the sun
  2 The sun is made up of these.
  3 winter, spring, summer, or fall

| Total Problems: | Total Correct: | Score: |

Read the passage and the questions that follow. Circle the letter beside the correct answer.

Something Sweet

Whether it is from sugar cane or sugar beets, it may wind up in a sugar bowl one day. Sugar is a popular and tasty food and the United States is a leading producer of raw sugar.

Raw sugar is obtained through a process that purifies the plant into syrup, then dehydrates the liquid so crystals will form. Though some crystals form in the liquid, the liquid is still suitable for use in some foods. When the crystals are removed, raw sucrose remains.

In order for this liquid to be made into white table sugar, more steps are involved. The liquid's molasses film is removed, the crystals are dissolved in water, and then filtered and evaporated. A final step involves spinning the filtered liquid at a very high speed which causes crystals to form. When dried, the crystals become the white granules that we use at home.

Sugar products and refined sugar have been around for many years. However, the process of refining sugar has become more efficient and widespread with the help of technology. So, the next time you eat a piece of candy or taste a slice of pie, remember that sweet taste is most likely from the special ingredient called sugar.

1. Raw sugar is made from:
    A. sugar beets
    B. sugar cane
    C. molasses
    D. both A and B

2. The United States is a leading producer of:
    A. sugar cane
    B. raw sugar
    C. refined sugar
    D. molasses

3. Making white table sugar basically involves:
    A. film removed, crystals dissolved, evaporation, spinning
    B. crystals added, film removed, water added
    C. evaporation, crystals dissolved, filtered
    D. filtering, molasses added, granules removed

4. Some foods use a liquid form of sugar:
    A. true
    B. false

| **Total Problems:**   **Total Correct:**   **Score:** |

Refer to the passage on page 42 to solve this puzzle.

Something Sweet Crossword Puzzle

Across

2   a liquid form of sugar

4   sugar that is not refined

7   a country that is a leading producer of raw sugar (two words)

9   sugar _____ (rhymes with feet)

10   refined sugar is this color

Down

1   a sweet film that covers the liquid sucrose

3   a tiny grain of sugar is called this

5   a household container, designed to hold refined sugar (two words)

6   sugar _____ (rhymes with rain)

8   the taste of sugar

Total Problems:	Total Correct:	Score:

Read the passage and answer the questions on the following page.

A Day at the Park

Ted and James were playing ball at the park in their neighborhood when they heard a faint whimper in the distance. The boys continued their game of catch, and later took turns pitching to each other. They were certain that Coach Brown was going to be impressed with their improvement. As it was time for them to gather their things and go home, the boys walked to the large oak tree to retrieve their bikes. There, they heard the whimpering sound again. Puzzled, the two boys began looking to see from where the small sound might be coming.

Ted searched in one direction and James went in another. One more time the small sound made its presence. It was practically right under James. He bent down and began searching through the leaves and brush. To his surprise he uncovered a small, fluffy, gray kitten. He began talking softly to the kitten and assured him everything was going to be okay. The poor animal seemed terribly frightened.

James called for Ted to let him know he had discovered a kitten, and that's where the sound was coming from in the woods. Ted was surprised to see the tiny little animal so scared and alone. The boys decided to take the kitten home. Dr. Davis, Ted's father, was a veterinarian, so he would be able to tell if the little kitten was in good health. Ted put the kitten in his large pocket on the front of his coat and off they went.

They arrived at Ted's house and quickly found Dr. Davis. The boys told him all about the visit to the park and how they found the kitten. Dr. Davis took the little kitten and began looking it over very carefully. He seemed to think the kitten was in pretty good health. He was most likely hungry and thirsty. James filled a bowl with water and Ted got a can of cat food. The little kitten slowly began eating and drinking. After a few minutes, the kitten curled up into a gray ball and went to sleep.

James and Ted asked if they would be able to keep the kitten. Dr. Davis felt like that would be okay, but if they heard of a lost gray kitten, they would have to give him up. The boys understood and they stayed by the side of their new furry friend the rest of the day. The day of ball practice really took a different turn that day for Ted and James.

Read each question. Circle the letter beside the correct answer.

1. What did James and Ted find at the park?
    A.   a baseball
    B.   a pile of leaves
    C.   a boy
    D.   a kitten

2. What made the boys think there was something in the woods?
    A.   They saw something move.
    B.   They heard a sound.
    C.   Someone told them about it.
    D.   They saw it wander into the woods.

3. How did the kitten get to Ted's house?
    A.   He rode in Ted's pocket.
    B.   James carried him.
    C.   Dr. Davis picked him up.
    D.   Coach Brown let him ride in the car.

4. Who did the boys ask to examine the kitten?
    A.   Mrs. Davis
    B.   James's father
    C.   Ted's father
    D.   Coach Brown

5. What did the kitten need?
    A.   milk   B.   a bath
    C.   food and water   D.   its mother

6. What were the boys planning to do with the kitten?
    A.   sell the kitten to a good home
    B.   keep it and take care of it
    C.   give the kitten to Dr. Davis
    D.   they didn't know

7. Why did the boys go to the park?
    A.   They had a baseball game.
    B.   They were looking for something Ted had lost.
    C.   They were practicing pitching and hitting.
    D.   They were riding their bikes.

Read the passage and the questions that follow. Circle the letter beside the correct answer.

Two Girls Having Fun

Most Saturday nights, Laura and Mei Li go to the theater to see a movie. The girls are best friends and have always enjoyed watching movies. Laura chooses the movie one week, and Mei Li will choose the next week's movie. The girls started their tradition while they were in the fourth grade. Now that they are in the fifth grade, they hope to continue for as long as they can.

Usually Mei Li's mother, Mrs. Kim, takes the girls to the theater. While the girls are watching the movie, Mrs. Kim goes to the jewelry store next door, which is owned by her sister. Mrs. Kim waits for the girls at the store and uses the time to visit her sister. After the movie, the girls go to the jewelry store to find Mrs. Kim.

Laura and Mei Li love to pretend they are rich ladies shopping for diamonds when they go to the jewelry store. They often act silly and begin laughing at themselves. However, they never do it when the store is open since that would be distracting to real customers.

Laura and Mei Li have a special friendship and they hope to find even more fun things to do together in the future. But for now, it is fun being best friends and movie pals.

1. What do Laura and Mei Li do for fun?
   A. watch movies and pretend to be rich ladies shopping
   B. pretend to be movie stars walking into a famous place
   C. make jewelry and wear expensive clothes
   D. look for hidden treasures

2. Where does Mrs. Kim's sister work?
   A. the movie theater
   B. a jewelry store
   C. a grocery store
   D. a clothing store

3. When do the girls go to the movies?
   A. Fridays
   B. Thursdays
   C. Sundays
   D. Saturdays

Total Problems: _____   Total Correct: _____   Score: _____

Refer to the passage on page 46 to solve this puzzle.

Two Girls Having Fun Crossword Puzzle

Across

1 the grade Laura and Mei Li are in
3 the type of jewelry the girls pretend to shop for
6 the name of the building where movies are shown

Down

1 Mei Li and Laura are best _____
2 the type of store Mrs. Kim's sister owns
4 the girls see one _____ most weeks
5 most Saturday _____ the girls go to the movies

Read the passage and answer the questions on the following page.

Morris and Dave

Dave was a normal twelve-year-old boy living in a small town who wanted fun things to do after school each day. He didn't have any brothers or sisters to play with like other kids. Dave didn't play on a sports team, take horseback riding lessons, or even have a hobby. Once his homework was done, he would either watch television or read a book. He was convinced his life was the most boring life any kid could have.

Dave's grandfather lived in the house next door. Sometimes Dave would go to his house and talk while his grandfather fed or brushed his horses. Dave loved his grandfather very much. He liked listening to his grandfather tell interesting stories. One day Dave went to his grandfather's farm and noticed a small dog was in the horse paddock running between the horse's legs. The horses did not seem bothered by the little dog, but occasionally they would kick their hind legs up to try to trip him. The horse's size did not seem to frighten the little guy at all. The dog was so quick that the movements and kicks of the horses were not hard for him to dodge.

Dave's grandfather explained that the little dog wandered up a few days ago. He figured the little dog was lost or had run away. Dave played with him for a while and begged his grandfather to let him keep the dog and care for him. His grandfather agreed and they became great friends.

The dog became known as Morris and he always kept the three horses—Timothy, Sally, and Duke—well entertained. From then on, every day after school Dave had something to which he looked forward. He could not wait to get off the bus and meet Morris in the field between the two houses. Dave was confident that he and Morris would be good friends for a very long time.

Read each question. Circle the letter beside the correct answer.

1. What did Dave usually do after school?
   A. watch TV
   B. play football
   C. go swimming
   D. build things

2. Why did Dave like visiting his grandfather?
   A. He liked helping care for the horses and the barn.
   B. He liked hearing his grandfather's stories.
   C. He liked making things with his grandfather.
   D. He liked working for his grandfather for extra money.

3. What did Dave find one day in the paddock?
   A. a horse
   B. a bird
   C. a dog
   D. a cat

4. Where was Dave's house?
   A. next to the school
   B. near the train tracks
   C. next to his grandfather's
   D. next to the library

5. What did Dave get that made him happy and no longer bored?
   A. Daisy
   B. Sally
   C. Duke
   D. Morris

Read the passage and answer the questions on the following page.

The Town of Bakersville

Mr. Leonard had worked for the fire department for many years. The people in the community were always happy to see Mr. Leonard in the big, red fire truck because they knew he was helping take care of the community. Bakersville was a small town with a big heart, people often said. People in this town really cared about one another.

One day, Mr. Leonard and his firemen were called to a fire. The call was about a small building that had caught fire from a nearby electrical pole. The building was a small pizza restaurant owned by a friend of Mr. Leonard's, Carl Jones. The fire truck raced to the little building and Mr. Leonard and his crew jumped off and began putting out the flames. Soon, the flames were out and the building was black from the burn. Fortunately, no one was inside.

Mr. Leonard stood in front of the building talking to Mr. Jones when suddenly they were both knocked over a distance of several feet and fell to the ground. Then a loud thud hit the ground and shook the earth. Stunned by the assault, the men looked up just in time to see Jason, Mr. Jones's son, standing over them. He pointed to where the men were standing and there was the burned electrical pole on the ground. The pole had fallen and the men didn't know it. Jason had shoved them out of the way just in time.

Gradually, the men gathered themselves and stood up to look at the accident. They thanked Jason for seeing the danger headed their way and helping them get out of its path. On the way to the fire truck, Mr. Leonard told Jason it was great to live in Bakersville where people are friendly enough to knock someone down whenever it is necessary. The men laughed and Mr. Leonard and his crew loaded up the truck and headed back to the station.

Read each question. Circle the letter beside the correct answer.

1. What job did Mr. Leonard have?
   A. policeman
   C. fireman
   B. restaurant owner
   D. banker

2. Where did the fire crew have to go to answer a call?
   A. a store
   B. a restaurant
   C. a house
   D. a school

3. Why did Mr. Leonard and Mr. Jones get knocked down after the fire was out?
   A. A tree fell on them.
   B. A boy pushed them.
   C. A truck was going to hit them.
   D. A dog was chasing them.

4. What caused the fire to start?
   A. an electrical pole
   B. An oven was left on.
   C. A candle was left burning.
   D. a fire from another building

5. What were the townspeople's attitudes toward each other?
   A. They were usually mean to each other for no reason.
   B. They were kind and cared for others.
   C. They were always trying to start fires in town.
   D. They were very private and didn't talk much to anyone.

6. Who was inside the burning building?
   A. Mr. Jones
   B. the crew
   C. Jason
   D. no one

7. Why was it good for Mr. Jones and Mr. Leonard to be knocked down by Jason?
   A. They were in the way of the fire truck.
   B. They were about to run into the burning building.
   C. They were about to get wet.
   D. They were in the path of a falling pole.

Total Problems: ___   Total Correct: ___   Score: ___

Read the passage and answer the questions on the following page.

Melanie Plays Golf

One day Melanie's father came home from work with a long box in his arms. He called for her to come to the family room and see what he had. She came immediately and saw the box. "What's in the box?" she asked.

"Well, that's for you to find out. Here open it and see," replied her dad.

Melanie opened the box and pulled out a long, straight, silver stick. As she pulled it completely out she noticed that it was a golf club. Happily, Melanie took the club and began practicing her stance and a slow golf swing.

"Is this for me?" asked Melanie.

"Yes, it is. I noticed you had a really good time last week at the miniature golf course so I thought you might like to try a real golf course with me sometime," said her father.

"I'd like that a lot. I think if I practice I could be really good," she said.

"Sure you could," her father continued. "All it takes is a little skill and a lot of practice. Golf is a very interesting sport. Your mom and I would like to play more often."

"Hey, Dad," exclaimed Melanie, "Could we go play for a while this Saturday?"

"Yes, in fact I was already planning on it," he said.

"Great!" said Melanie, as she skipped out of the room, cheering.

Read each question. Circle the letter beside the correct answer.

1. Why was Melanie so excited?
   A. Her father had just come home from work.
   B. Her package had come in the mail.
   C. Her dad planned to take her to play golf.
   D. Her mom was giving her golf lessons.

2. Where was Melanie when she got her new club?
   A. at home
   B. at the miniature golf course
   C. at a party
   D. at school

3. When was the golf day going to be?
   A. Tuesday
   B. Friday
   C. Saturday
   D. Sunday

4. Who likes golf in Melanie's family?
   A. Mom and Dad
   B. only Dad
   C. Dad and Melanie
   D. Mom, Dad, and Melanie

5. How did Melanie feel about the surprise?
   A. very excited
   B. disappointed
   C. confused
   D. uncertain

6. For what occasion did Melanie get the surprise?
   A. no special occasion
   B. birthday
   C. end of school
   D. Valentine's Day

Read the passage and answer the questions on the following page.

Turning Twelve

Mark was turning twelve on Friday. He and his mom had planned his birthday party two weeks ago. He was having six fiends come home with him after school and spend the night. Jake, Joel, Frank, Matt, Chad, and Hugo were all coming to Mark's house. First, they would play in the backyard, and then they would have hot dogs and birthday cake. Mark was also very excited about getting to stay up as late as he and his friends wanted. It was going to be the best birthday ever!

As soon as the bus stopped at his house, the fun began. All seven boys jumped off the bus, went inside Mark's house, and put away their things. Mark's mother had popcorn and soda ready for snacks, and she even allowed them to watch a few cartoons while they ate. Soon the boys were in the backyard having fun.

After three hours of playing tag in the yard, telling jokes, and exploring Mark's new tree house, the group headed inside for dinner. Mark's dad grilled hot dogs for everyone. For dessert, there was, of course, cake and ice cream. Soon everyone was very full and getting tired. Mark opened his gifts and then suggested they watch a movie. Everyone was so exhausted. The movie had been on for only twenty-five minutes when all seven boys fell sound asleep.

The next morning the boys woke up and resumed their activities. First to the tree house, then to the garage for bikes, skateboards, and in-line skates. Mark's mom came out with a tray of hot muffins and juice for everyone for breakfast. Quickly, each one of them ate and, of course, continued playing. At eleven o'clock, several of the boys' mothers were arriving to pick them up. After everyone had gone, Mark thanked his mom for a wonderful birthday party. She smiled and said it was fun for her too. Mark admitted that the party was great fun, but the best thing is that he is now twelve years old.

Read each question. Circle the letter beside the correct answer.

1. Who was having a birthday party?
    A.   Frank
    B.   Matt
    C.   Mark
    D.   Jake

2. Where did the boys play after school?
    A.   in the house
    B.   in the backyard
    C.   in the garage
    D.   in Mark's room

3. Who met the boys at home after school?
    A.   Mark's mom
    B.   Mark's dad
    C.   Mark's grandmother
    D.   Mark's best friend

4. What did the boys do after eating dinner?
    A.   play in the backyard
    B.   watch a movie
    C.   do homework
    D.   explore the neighborhood

5. What did the boys have to eat that night?
    A.   popcorn
    B.   pizza
    C.   candy
    D.   hot dogs

6. When did the boys begin going home the next day?
    A.   12 o'clock
    B.   10 o'clock
    C.   11 o'clock
    D.   1 o'clock

Total Problems:	Total Correct:	Score:

Refer to the passage on page 54 to solve this puzzle.

Turning Twelve Puzzle

Across

2 Mark's mom made these for breakfast.

4 an outside toy one can ride on after pushing off

6 the time of day the guests went home (not afternoon or evening)

8 Instead of watching the entire movie, the boys went to _____.

9 the structure in the backyard that interested the boys

Down

1 You can ride this if you pedal and keep your balance.

2 the person who was having the party

3 Hot and crunchy, it's often sold at the movies.

5 the age Mark turned on this birthday

7 They had this along with the cake.

Total Problems: ___   Total Correct: ___   Score: ___

Read the passage and answer the questions that follow. Circle the letter beside the correct answer.

The Happy Dragon

Wendy Chen lives with her parents in the suburbs of a large city. Right before Wendy was born, her parents, Mr. and Mrs. Chen, moved to the United States from China. The Chens like America very much.

The Happy Dragon is the Chen's restaurant. Mr. and Mrs. Chen are both very good at making delicious Chinese foods. Mrs. Chen usually helps take care of the customers in the dining room, while Mr. Chen almost always works in the kitchen preparing food.

Wendy has been going to the restaurant with her parents all her life. She is now old enough to help at the restaurant. Each time customers sit down at a table, Wendy brings them ice water, hot tea, and fried noodles. Eventually, Wendy will take orders and be a waitress at the restaurant.

At school, Wendy's friends ask her lots of questions about the restaurant and Chinese food. Wendy likes to talk about the restaurant because she is proud of it and her parents. Many of her friends enjoy eating there with their families.

1. From where did the Chens immigrate?
   A. Norway
   B. Japan
   C. China
   D. Canada

2. What do Wendy's parents do for work?
   A. They own a restaurant.
   B. They are teachers.
   C. They build large houses.
   D. They have a movie theater.

3. How long has Wendy been going to the restaurant?
   A. about two years
   B. only three months
   C. all her life
   D. less than four years

4. When did Mr. and Mrs. Chen leave their native country?
   A. after Wendy was born
   B. before Wendy was born
   C. two years ago
   D. when they were little

Total Problems: _____ Total Correct: _____ Score: _____

Read the passage and answer the questions on the following page.

Neil's Big Game

Neil went to bed exhausted after a very busy day. He had been to school, baseball practice, and a birthday party for his friend James. As soon as he crawled in bed, he immediately dropped off to sleep.

During the night, Neil began to dream. His mind took him to Dodger Stadium in May where the Major League baseball season was in full swing. Neil dreamed he was sitting on the bench in the dugout, right beside some of the biggest names in baseball. The game was in the third inning and the score was tied three to three.

Suddenly, the Dodgers' manager came over to Neil and told him he was in the lineup. Neil was shocked! He couldn't believe he was about to bat at Dodger Stadium. He took his place in the on deck circle to warm up and began stretching and practicing his swing.

Minutes later he was at the plate. The first pitch came in low and fast. Neil swung and "crack"—his bat nailed the ball. It was a line drive to left field. Neil felt stuck for a second as he looked at what he had just done. A loud roar came from the Dodgers' dugout and off went Neil to first base.

The ball seemed to fly toward first base like a torpedo. Neil raced for the bag and his toes touched one second before the catch was made. He was safe! What a wonderful feeling! Neil happily let out a yell in celebration of his success.

Just then Neil opened his eyes. He was not in Dodger Stadium. He was lying in his bed! Wow, what a dream! Stunned by the reality the dream seemed to have, he sat up in his bed for a few minutes to savor the memory of being a Major League baseball player.

Read each question. Circle the letter beside the correct answer.

1. Why did Neil go to bed quickly?
    A.   He was in trouble.
    B.   He was very tired.
    C.   He had to get up early the next day.
    D.   It was getting late.

2. What did Neil do during the night?
    A.   He fell out of the bed.
    B.   His blanket came off.
    C.   He had a dream.
    D.   He snored very loudly.

3. What did Neil dream he was doing?
    A.   He dreamed he was playing in a Major League baseball game.
    B.   He dreamed he was flying off a very high cliff.
    C.   He dreamed he was sleeping in his bed.
    D.   He dreamed he was falling from a cloud.

4. Where was Neil in reality?
    A.   at a baseball game
    B.   at home in his bed
    C.   at a carnival
    D.   at school in his classroom

5. Why did Neil seem shocked when he heard a loud "crack"?
    A.   He was scared that a tree was falling on top of him.
    B.   He was surprised that the weather was getting so bad.
    C.   He was amazed that he hit the ball so far.
    D.   He was upset because he broke his mother's vase.

Read the passage and answer the questions on the following page.

Nancy's Help

Nancy was up early on Saturday to help her father with an important job. They were going to paint the fence in the yard. Mr. Bickers, Nancy's father, had gotten all the supplies the day before. So, everything was all ready to go.

After breakfast, Nancy and her father went outside to begin their work. They carried out buckets of paint, brushes, and cloths. Nancy helped her father open the paint cans and place all of the supplies around the work area. Next, they opened the paint cans and began working. Nancy was impressed by how nice it looked when they spread the clean white paint over the dull gray wood. This was going to make their yard look beautiful in spring with the green grass, colorful flowers, and white fence.

The painters worked for several minutes when Nancy's mom came to tell her husband of a phone call. Mr. Bickers went inside to take the call and soon returned to tell Nancy that he would be gone a few minutes longer. He encouraged her to continue working and he would return shortly. Nancy nodded and kept painting. In fact she kept painting until she had completed the entire front yard side of the fence.

About thirty minutes later, Nancy's father returned. He was very surprised at her progress. Nancy had really done a lot of work! Mr. Bickers hugged his daughter and thanked her for doing such a great job. Nancy smiled and said it was okay because she had fun doing it. The rest of the afternoon the two partners worked on completing the project. Tired and splotched with paint drops, the pair finally finished their masterpiece at 4:00 p.m.

To admire their work, they decided to prepare glasses of fresh lemonade, sit on the porch, and watch the sun go down. That was really a day's work. Mr. Bickers and his number one painting partner had done an excellent job.

Name _____

Read each question. Circle the letter beside the correct answer.

1. What was Nancy going to help her father do?
    A. wash the dog
    B. paint the house
    C. paint the fence
    D. make lemonade

2. Why did Nancy have to work alone for awhile?
    A. Her father wanted to see how much she could do by herself.
    B. Mrs. Bickers needed to see Nancy's father for a few minutes.
    C. Mr. Bickers received a phone call.
    D. They ran out of supplies and her father went to get more.

3. How did Nancy's father react when he returned?
    A. He was surprised that she had done so much work.
    B. He was disappointed that she was not all finished.
    C. He was tired and wanted to stop for the day.
    D. He was worried that it might start to rain.

4. What did Nancy and her father do to celebrate?
    A. They went out to dinner that evening with Nancy's mom.
    B. Nancy's dad bought her a surprise.
    C. They sat on the porch with lemonade and looked at their work.
    D. They decided to become professional fence painters to make money.

5. What does the author mean by the use of the word "masterpiece"?
    A. Every time someone paints they create a masterpiece.
    B. Painted works of art are sometimes called masterpieces.
    C. Working outside painting houses and fences is often called masterpiece work.
    D. Masterpieces are usually artistic paintings that are painted white like their fence.

Total Problems: Total Correct: Score:

Name _____

Read the passage and the statements that follow. Decide if each statement is true or false. Place a T or F in the blank next to each statement.

Catherine's Catch

It was the first day of basketball season and Catherine was on the team! She had been looking forward to the chance to play on the all-girl team for two years. Finally, it was here and she was ready. Practices had started over two weeks ago and now it was time for the first game. She proudly dressed in her gold and white Eagles jersey and shorts to join her team at the school gymnasium.

Catherine was one of the first team members to arrive. She went to the locker room to put away her things. She soon found a few friends and began practicing drills with them. In a little while, the entire team was there and the coach was giving his pregame talk. He talked about how careful they needed to be in the game. The other team, the Pirates, is very good and it is hard to get the ball away from them. Coach Bryan told the team that a win was possible, as long as everyone would concentrate.

The horn sounded and the teams took the court. The first play of the game was a clear shot from center court to the net from the Pirates team. The shot would have been perfect, but the ball moved and the goal was missed. Lisa, Catherine's best friend, caught the ball, tossed it to Catherine for a lay up and two points were now on the board for the Eagles!

The Pirates took possession of the ball as well as the score board for the rest of the first half. Then, the Eagles came on to claim victory! Catherine was pleased with her team's performance. And she was especially pleased with her own. This was going to be a great season!

1. _____ Catherine is on the Eagle's team.

2. _____ The team had not practiced before the game.

3. _____ The Pirates were a tough team to beat.

4. _____ Most of the players on the teams were boys.

5. _____ Coach Bryan was Catherine's father.

6. _____ The first shot by the Eagles scored two points.

7. _____ The Pirates won the game.

Total Problems: _____ Total Correct: _____ Score: _____

Refer to the passage on page 62 to solve this puzzle.

Catherine's Catch Crossword Puzzle

Across

2 the team Catherine's team played against
3 the period of months a sport is played
8 an area for players to store their things and change clothes (two words)
9 the opposite of lose
10 the Eagle's coach (his last name)

Down

1 the name of Catherine's team
4 the large (usually lighted) screen that displays the scores
5 the name of the uniform shirt
6 an enclosed area often used for indoor school sports
7 an organized group of players for a sport

| Total Problems: | Total Correct: | Score: |

Read the passage and answer the questions on the following page.

Natalia's Place

"I need someone to take care of Natalia for a few weeks," she heard her father say. "Her mother is sick, and I need to take care of her as she recovers."

Natalia crept back into her bedroom. Early the next morning her father awakened her. "Natalia, Aunt Becca is here to take you home with her."

Natalia knew she would miss her parents and didn't want to go away and stay in a strange place, though she had visited there once before. She remembered Florence, her cousin. Florence was mature for her age, and said, "My name is Florence. Friends call me 'Flo' for short."

She was glad to see Florence's big smile and open arms. One day Florence said, "Come quickly, Natalia. I have something to show you."

The two girls raced across a field of wildflowers and into the woods. Down a steep bank they skidded and landed feet first beside a little brook. "Look Natalia," said Florence. "I made this myself." There in the stream was a water wheel made from branches and wooden blades. Each piece was fitted perfectly together and turned smoothly in the clear, cool stream.

"What does it do?" asked Natalia.

"Oh, it doesn't *do* anything. It is just to enjoy. I like to watch the water flow by, and listen to the wheel go 'slap, slap, slap' as it turns in the stream. It is peaceful, and reminds me that life is good, but that it takes a lot of cooperation to make it so. You know, the branches, the wooden paddles, the brook, and of course, my handiwork!" They both laughed. It was the first time Natalia had laughed since she had left home.

The girls visited the little brook whenever they had a chance to relax. Often Natalia would just lie on her back, watching the green leaves above, and listening to the slap, slap, slap of the little wheel in the brook. Whenever she missed her family, she would think that she was doing her part to help her mother by staying with Florence for a while.

When her mother got well and she returned home, Natalia told her mother of the little brook. "I called it Natalia's place," she said. "Whenever I felt lonely, I would go there and remember that life is good, but that it takes a lot of cooperation to make it so."

"Maybe one day you will take me to Natalia's place," her mother said, as she hugged and kissed her. "I'm glad you were with Florence while I was recovering."

Read each question. Circle the letter beside the correct answer.

1. Why did Natalia have to go away?
   A. Her father had to work.
   B. Her mother was sick.
   C. Her cousin was very lonely.
   D. She was on a vacation.

2. What did Natalia think about leaving home?
   A. She didn't want to go because she would miss her parents.
   B. She was scared of airplanes.
   C. She was excited and begged to go.
   D. She was unhappy and refused to go.

3. What did Flo show her cousin?
   A. a water wheel
   B. a tree house
   C. a trail in the woods
   D. her new dollhouse

4. When do Flo and Natalia visit the brook?
   A. when they are hiding from Flo's little brother
   B. when they have a chance to relax
   C. when it is almost time to go eat supper
   D. when it is summer and they have free time

5. What could Florence mean by the phrase "it takes a lot of cooperation to make it so"?
   A. People need each other during difficult times in life.
   B. The water wheel has different parts that work together.
   C. Florence needed help making the water wheel.
   D. Natalia should cooperate more with her mother.

Name _____

Read the passage and answer the questions on the following page.

Katia's Airplane Ride

Katia's father is an airline pilot who flies all over the world. Sometimes he is gone for weeks at the time. One day when Katia came home from school her father said, "Katia, I have a surprise for you."

Katia was excited. "What is it?" she cried.

"It will have to wait until tomorrow," her father said.

The next day was Saturday. Katia was up at dawn. In the kitchen, her father had fixed a big breakfast. "We have to eat a big breakfast for our surprise today," he said.

Katia and her father drove out of town to a small airport. There were several small airplanes parked near the little hangar.

"Katia," her father said. "You have always wanted to ride in an airplane. I have an even better surprise. You will ride and you will also fly the airplane today. That is, if you want to."

"Do I want to?" Katia exclaimed. "That has always been my dream."

Katia walked quickly to a small blue and white, single engine airplane with her father. Her father explained each thing he did as they prepared to fly. Once in the air, Katia gazed out the window. "It is beautiful," she said. "I love it up here!"

"Now, Katia," said her father, "it is your turn to fly. Just do what I say, and you will be fine. These are dual controls, so I will be your backup at all times."

At first they just flew straight and level. Then, her father said, "How about a turn or two?"

"Let's do it!" Katia said.

Much too soon, Katia saw the airport come into view. "Do we have to land now?" she asked. "I'm afraid so," her father said. "We only have the airplane for one hour. But how about doing this again?"

"Do you have to ask?" Katia asked with a twinkle in her eye. "I can hardly wait."

"Well," her father said with a big grin, "I think I have a budding pilot on my hands."

Read each question. Circle the letter beside the correct answer.

1. Why did Katia get up early the morning of the surprise?
   A. She was so excited about the airplane trip.
   B. She wanted to find out what the surprise was.
   C. She wanted to help her mother make breakfast.
   D. She hoped her parents were getting her a pony.

2. Where did Katia's father take her?
   A. to the airport where he works
   B. to a small airport out of town
   C. to an airplane museum
   D. to an amusement park with plane rides

3. What had always been Katia's dream?
   A. to ride in an airplane
   B. to pretend she was a bird
   C. to see a real airport
   D. to fly an airplane

4. How long was Katia's airplane ride?
   A. two hours
   B. one hour
   C. three hours
   D. four hours

5. How was Katia's father able to control the plane even while Katia was using her controls?
   A. The airplane just knew who was the real pilot.
   B. The airplane was not really controlled by Katia's controls.
   C. The airplane had dual controls.
   D. The airplane was not going fast enough for the controls to work.

6. What did Katia say about doing this event another time?
   A. no
   B. maybe
   C. She was too scared to say.
   D. yes

Total Problems:	Total Correct:	Score:

67

Name _____

Read the passage and answer the questions on the following page.

The Train

Only four months ago my family moved to a new house. It is a nice house and has lots of space for our family of five, but it doesn't seem like home yet. Our old house was much closer to town and we lived near the railroad tracks. The train would come by almost every hour and blow its horn. My sister, Leigh, and I would stand in our backyard and wave to the conductor as the enormous engine passed us. Our new house is far from any railroads, streets, or other houses. My parents say they like the privacy of the new house, but I miss the excitement of the old place.

I remember when we first moved to the old house and the train would often scare me at night. But, in only a few weeks I was used to the horn and I began to anticipate the rhythmic clatter of the wheels on the tracks. It was home and I miss it now. So many days after school, I would lie in the grass in the backyard and stare at the clouds, thinking. Then I would feel the vibration of the train's approach and soon the horn would sound. I would sit up and scream at the top of my voice, only to be drowned out by the sound of the horn. I was amazed by the way the sounds were mixing together, and the stronger sound was the only one to be heard.

I guess those days are gone now and I will begin to discover new things that are unique about our new house. I will miss the old house and neighborhood. But, now that we are here, Leigh and I love playing in the giant backyard and running as fast as we can over the grassy hill in the corner of the yard. I think this place will become a favorite as well. The clouds are certainly easy to see out here. And I still love to lie on the grass and just think about things.

Name _____

Read each question and write your answer in the space provided.

1. What is the main idea of this story? _____

_____

_____

_____

2. What does the narrator miss about the old house? _____

_____

_____

_____

3. Why was the narrator amazed by the train's horn and its loudness? _____

_____

_____

_____

4. Who enjoyed running on the grassy hill in the new house's yard? _____

_____

_____

_____

5. Where would the person telling the story do a lot of thinking? _____

_____

_____

_____

Total Problems:	Total Correct:	Score:

Read the passage and answer the questions on the following page.

Mr. Borg Visits Russia

In early spring, Mr. Borg visited St. Petersburg, Russia. As the airplane landed, he saw large patches of snow among the leafless birch trees. The airport had been cleared of snow, but the weather was still too cold for leaves and blossoms.

As the bus crossed the river, Mr. Borg saw an icebreaker ship opening the way for shipping traffic. He had never seen an icebreaker at work before. The bus stopped at a beautiful museum called "The Hermitage," built by Peter the Great, a Russian emperor.

As Mr. Borg toured the Hermitage, he saw a group of school children and a teacher on a field trip. Right away, the children recognized Mr. Borg's strange accent. They crowded around him chattering in Russian.

One of the girls spoke English. "Are you an American?" she asked. "Yes, I am," he said. "Oh, good. My name is Irina. My friends want me to ask you some questions. May I?" she asked. "Of course," he replied.

"What is your name?" Irina asked

"My name is Walter Borg," he said. Irina translated as Mr. Borg spoke.

"Where do you live?" she asked.

"I live in the United States of America, in a state called Georgia," he said.

"Do you have a dog?" Irina asked.

"Yes, I have two dogs. They are Brittany and Dolly."

When Irina translated, a boy asked, "How big are they?"

"They are this big," Mr Borg said, holding his hands about ten inches apart.

The teacher hurried over and spoke some excited words in Russian.

"What did she say?" Mr. Borg asked.

"We have to hurry now. We are late for the next tour," Irina said. "May we have your autograph?"

Mr. Borg signed autographs as the children crowded around. The teacher led the children on through the Hermitage. Irina turned back and said, "Thank you for talking with us. You gave me a chance to practice my English."

Read each question. Circle the letter beside the correct answer.

1. What kind of weather does Russia have in Spring?
   A. hot
   B. snowy
   C. rainy
   D. dry

2. With whom did Mr. Borg talk at the museum?
   A. an American
   B. Irina
   C. a teacher
   D. a tour guide

3. Who was Peter the Great?
   A. He was a great writer in Russia.
   B. He was the president of Russia.
   C. He was a famous emperor of Russia.
   D. He worked at the museum.

4. Why did Mr. Borg tell about his dogs?
   A. The children asked him about them.
   B. People saw them while he was walking.
   C. His dogs looked like the ones in the paintings.
   D. He didn't talk about his dogs.

5. Why did Irina's teacher hurry the children along?
   A. Because they were going to be late for the movie.
   B. Because they were leaving the museum and the buses were leaving.
   C. Because their tour was about to begin.
   D. Because they were not eating their lunches fast enough.

6. How did Mr. Borg travel to Russia for his visit?
   A. car   B. airplane
   C. boat   D. train

7. For what did Irina thank Mr. Borg before she left?
   A. She thanked him for talking to her so she could practice her English.
   B. She thanked him for giving her some candy.
   C. She thanked him for helping her find her teacher.
   D. She thanked him for sharing his lunch with her.

Total Problems:	Total Correct:	Score:

Refer to the passage on page 70 to solve this puzzle.

Mr. Borg Visits Russia Crossword Puzzle

Across
5   What city was Mr. Borg visiting?
9   What was on the ground in large patches?
10 The children asked Mr. Borg to give them this.

Down
1   What kind of pets does Mr. Borg own?
2   What nationality is Mr. Borg?
3   Who was the school girl who spoke English?
4   This means to change words to a different language.
6   What museum did Mr. Borg visit?
7   Mr. Borg has a dog with this name.
8   Mr. Borg lives in this state.

Total Problems: _____   Total Correct: _____   Score: _____

Read the passage and answer the questions on the following page.

A Camping Trip

Juan and his brother Mark wanted to go camping. Their mother, Mrs. Gomez, said, "I'll take you if your school work is completed and done well."

"Oh, great!" they said in one voice.

"We'll work hard. We promise!" Juan said.

Finally the day came for the camping trip. Each day after school, Mrs. Gomez had taken the boys to a store to get items on the checklist she had helped them to prepare: food, water, repair kits for camp gear, fuel for the camp stove, more food, everything they would need for a weekend in the woods.

Friday afternoon, in a heavy rain, Mrs. Gomez and the boys loaded their gear and headed for the national park. Long before dark, the rain stopped and they set up camp and started a campfire. Mrs. Gomez had prepared "bucket stew" at home. When the fire was ablaze, she hung the stew pot over the flames and soon the wonderful aroma of "bucket stew" filled the campsite.

Early the next morning, Mrs. Gomez went to the dock to fish. The boys wanted to fix "fire toast." The first two slices of bread burned badly. Soon they learned to make crisp, brown "fire toast," covered in blackberry jam given to them by Grandmother Gomez.

There were plenty of fish for supper, for everyone had caught lots of fish that day. Mrs. Gomez even caught a large trout. "I'll prepare this one tonight and put it in the cooler. For breakfast tomorrow, it will be a real treat."

Soon, it was time to break camp and pack for home. Mrs. Gomez taught the boys how to clean their equipment and pack it for use the next time. Juan said, "I will be very careful with this equipment, because I want to be ready to go camping again soon." Mark said, "I have already started making a new checklist. I learned a lot on this trip."

As Mrs. Gomez drove home, both boys peppered her with questions about their next camping trip. "A couple more trips like this," she said, "and we'll be ready for a camping vacation in the mountains, or a canoe trip in Canada."

"All right!!" Mark said.

"Yes!" exclaimed Juan.

Read each question. Circle the letter beside the correct answer.

1. What did Mark and Juan want to do?
    A. go get camping supplies
    B. find hidden places in the woods
    C. go on a camping trip
    D. get a new pet

2. Who helped the boys get their camping items together?
    A. their father
    B. their mother
    C. Uncle Tom
    D. no one

3. Where did the boys choose to camp?
    A. in the backyard
    B. at a national park
    C. in a neighbor's field
    D. in the wooded area behind Grandpa's farm

4. What did the campers eat on their trip?
    A. hamburgers, hot dogs, and chips
    B. vegetables, seeds, and fruits
    C. water, energy bars, and milk shakes
    D. fish, stew, and bread

5. The camping equipment was going to be put away for what reason?
    A. for the next trip
    B. so the boys could return it to Mrs. Gomez
    C. for another group of campers
    D. because they didn't want it anymore

Total Problems: _____   Total Correct: _____   Score: _____

Refer to the passage on page 73 to solve this puzzle.

A Camping Trip Crossword Puzzle

Across

1   a source of heat for a campsite
3   where Mrs. Gomez went to fish
7   sweet stuff Grandmother Gomez made (two words)
8   needed to make the camp stove work

Down

2   the day after Thursday
4   a list that helps you pack necessary items for a trip
5   Mark's brother
6   type of fish Mrs. Gomez caught and cooked for breakfast
7   The boys burned this while making "fire toast."

Total Problems:	Total Correct:	Score:

Read the passage and answer the questions on the following page.

The Monkey Bars at Last!

Every Wednesday our physical education class doesn't go to the gym. Instead, we go to the playground for a physical fitness test. We all have to participate in order to earn free time afterwards, but the whole test is pretty fun. We start on the first set of equipment at the back of the playground and follow a path to each of the other activities. At the end we get our elapsed time from the coach's stopwatch.

I like the fitness course and I like to see if I can make it through the entire course faster each time I do it. Coach Warner says we are his best class for this activity. We begin with the long jump, then go to this wall we have to climb over, then swing across a puddle of water. The last few challenges are to jump in and out of tires lying on the ground, run diagonally back and forth through wooden pegs, and finally hit the monkey bars to swing into the finish line! It is a lot of fun to get to the monkey bars because you know you're finished at that point.

My best friend, Kathy, likes this fitness course, too. Ken, a boy in our class, is always trying to beat us and get a better time than ours. He has only beaten my time once, and that was because I lost my shoe as I was climbing over the wall. Kathy is very fast and Ken has never beaten her. I think that is great. She is a fast runner and her only competitor in running is Lee, another boy in our school. He is very fast, also.

We have only a few more Wednesdays left this year to do the fitness test, so we have to do our best each time. We certainly don't want anyone to break our records! Maybe next year we can get even better at it.

Read each statement. Decide if it is true or false. Place a T or F in the blank next to each statement.

1. _____ Ken is a faster runner than Kathy.

2. _____ The monkey bars are the last item on the fitness test.

3. _____ One challenge on the fitness test is to swing over a puddle of water.

4. _____ Coach Warner is the physical education teacher.

5. _____ The fitness tests are done on Tuesdays.

6. _____ Lee is not a very fast runner.

Read each question. Circle the letter beside the correct answer.

7. How many challenges are in the fitness test?
   - A. 5
   - B. 6
   - C. 7
   - D. 4

8. Where is the fitness test equipment located?
   - A. on the front of the playground
   - B. at the back of the playground
   - C. in the gymnasium
   - D. not given

9. Who is telling the story?
   - A. Kenny
   - B. Lee
   - C. Kathy's friend
   - D. Coach Warner

10. How do the students know how fast they complete the test?
    - A. The coach times them on his stopwatch.
    - B. The students time each other.
    - C. The students estimate the time mentally.
    - D. There is a clock in the gym that tells the time.

Total Problems: Total Correct: Score:

Refer to the passage on page 76 to solve this puzzle.

The Monkey Bars at Last Crossword Puzzle

Across

2   The narrator lost hers once climbing over the wall.
3   a common name for a leader of a sports team or physical education teacher
4   to get better with practice
6   the last item on the fitness test (two words)

Down

1   One event requires the runners to jump in and out of these.
2   a device used for timing things very precisely
3   The runners have to _____ over this wall in the test.
5   the boy in the school who can run the fastest

| Total Problems: | Total Correct: | Score: |

Answer Key

Reading Charts

Name _____

Use the information in the chart to answer the following questions.

Chart of Animal Colors for Class Play

Red	Blue	Green	Yellow
Bird	Fish	Frog	Bird
Fish	Bird	Bird	Fish
Dog	Dolphin	Lizard	Dog
Guinea Pig	Butterfly	Worm	Monkey

1. According to the chart, what are the possible colors for the fish? _red, blue, yellow_
2. Which animals can be green in the play? _frog, bird, lizard, worm_
3. Which animal can be any of the colors? _bird_
4. In the red group, which animals cannot fly? _fish, dog, guinea pig_
5. How many different colors can the fish be? _3_
6. How many colors can a dog be in the play? _2_
7. Which animal can only be yellow? _monkey_
8. How many different animals are there in all? _10_

© Carson-Dellosa CD-2204 Total Problems: Total Correct: Score: **9**

Reading Tables

Name _____

Use the information in the table to answer the following questions.

Camp Activities

Monday (a.m.)	Tuesday (a.m.)	Wednesday (a.m.)	Thursday (a.m.)	Friday (a.m.)
Crafts	Soccer	Hiking	Tennis	Rafting
Swimming	Swimming	Movies	Cooking	Movies
(p.m.)	**(p.m.)**	**(p.m.)**	**(p.m.)**	**(p.m.)**
Horseback riding	Tennis	Book club	Woodworking	Skating
Volleyball	Relay races	Aerobics	Swimming	Dancing
Beach trips	Shopping	Crafts	Shopping	Swimming
Biking	Cooking	Swimming	Rock climbing	Free time

1. What day(s) is soccer an option for the campers? _Tuesday_
2. What sedentary activity is scheduled for Wednesday mornings? _movies_
3. When is crafts offered in the afternoon? _Wednesday_
4. What activity is offered every day of the week? _swimming_
5. On what two days is cooking offered? _Tuesday, Thursday_
6. What ball sport(s) is/are offered on Monday? _volleyball_
7. When is free time offered? _Friday afternoon_
8. What activities are offered more than once during the week? _crafts, swimming, tennis, shopping, cooking, movies_
9. When is skating offered? _Friday afternoon_
10. Which day(s) has/have the most athletic activities offered? _Monday, Tuesday, Friday_

10 Total Problems: Total Correct: Score: © Carson-Dellosa CD-2204

Reading Graphs

Name _____

Use the information from the graph to answer the following questions.

Zoo Animals Counted by Mrs. Sullivan's Class

(bar graph: apes 15, seals 10, camels 5, birds 12, zebras 7, lions 2)

1. How many seals did the students see? _10_
2. How many more apes than camels were seen? _10_
3. Which animal was most numerous at the zoo? _apes_
4. How many zebras were there? _7_
5. What animal were there only 2 of at the zoo? _lions_
6. How many animals in all were seen by the students? _51_
7. How many birds were there? _12_
8. How many more zebras were seen than camels? _2_

© Carson-Dellosa CD-2204 Total Problems: Total Correct: Score: **11**

Sequence

Name _____

Read the passage. Determine the sequence of events and number the six statements in the order they occur in the passage.

Juan's Time Line

Juan was assigned a project in school that would require him to make a time line of his life. His teacher told the class to use a large poster to display the time line. The students were to use pictures of themselves to show each year of their lives from birth to present. With each year of their lives, there should also be a corresponding picture and written description of an event in the world.

This project meant Juan had to do some research. Juan took his assignment sheet and got a sheet of poster paper from the closet. He then drew a ten-year time line on the poster.

Next, he gathered research to provide the notable world events. He found some of the information on the Internet. He carefully wrote a description of each event on the poster. Finally, he pasted pictures of some world events on the poster. Now, Juan was finished with his project.

1. _5_ Juan wrote a brief description beside each picture.
2. _4_ He gathered information on notable events.
3. _6_ He pasted pictures of himself and famous events on his poster.
4. _3_ He drew a line for the time line that would represent 10 years.
5. _1_ Juan got an assignment for a time line from his teacher.
6. _2_ Juan got a piece of poster paper.

12 Total Problems: Total Correct: Score: © Carson-Dellosa CD-2204

© Carson-Dellosa CD-2204

79

Name _____   Sequence

Read the passage and each question that follows. Circle the letter beside the correct answer. Refer to the passage if necessary.

Learning to Swim

Margaret is an excellent swimmer. Many times people ask her how she became such a good swimmer. She always credits her early training in the water to her current success. Margaret tells people there are a few important steps to follow in learning to swim and appreciating the water, rather than fear it.

First, it is important for the swimmer to relax and put in his feet. Then, he should proceed to standing in shallow areas, wading in further as desired. As the water level reaches the legs, hips, and chest, the swimmer should push the water back and forth to feel the water. The swimmer can go deeper into the water letting the entire body be submerged, except for the head.

Then, standing in shallow water and holding onto something stable, the swimmer should take a deep breath and put his face in the water for a few seconds. After trying this a few times, the swimmer can try blowing out air to create bubbles in the water while his face is in the water.

Once a beginning swimmer has felt the sensation of water on his face and is no longer scared, he can try learning a few strokes. When learning strokes, it is important to practice first with only the hands and feet. Later, the swimmer can put his face in the water and try to move through the water rhythmically.

1. What is the first thing a beginning swimmer should do?
   A. put in his face
   (B) put in his feet
   C. learn the proper strokes
   D. wade into the deep end

2. What is necessary to do right before learning the strokes?
   A. splash the water with your hands
   B. stand in the shallow end
   (C) become used to the sensation of water on your face
   D. learn to dive correctly

3. What is the last step for a beginning swimmer?
   A. learning to call for the lifeguard
   B. learning to swim in competition
   C. learning to care for a drowning person
   (D) learning the strokes and moving the body

© Carson-Dellosa CD-2204   Total Problems: Total Correct: Score: **13**

Name _____   Finding the Main Idea

Read each passage and question. Circle the letter beside the correct answer.

Gravity

One day Dan and his father were talking about why things fall down when they are dropped. His father explained that the earth has a natural pull called gravity. Gravity pulls things on the Earth's surface toward the center of the Earth. Dan was confused. His father began showing him how objects are drawn or pulled toward the Earth's center. He demonstrated by rolling a ball down a hill. Then he showed Dan the leaves in the yard and reminded him that they just fell that way. The objects try to get to the lowest place possible. None can actually get to the Earth's center because it is covered by many other objects. Gravity is natural to us and we depend on it for many things we do

1. What is the main idea of this story?
   A. Earth
   (B) gravity
   C. falling
   D. atmosphere

The Circus

A girl went whirling up into the air and after doing two somersaults landed directly on the feet of the man lying on his back. Jan looked on in awe as the circus people completed one death-defying act after another. The circus amazed Jan. She liked the acrobats, the animals, and especially the happy feeling she got from being at the circus. The costumes were brightly colored and the tricks were dazzling. Going to the circus was exciting because it was different every year and the clowns always made Jan laugh. As Jan left the circus, she promised herself that she would be back again next year.

2. What is the main idea of this story?
   (A) Jan likes the circus.
   B. The circus is in town every year.
   C. The acrobats have improved.
   D. The animals are better every year.

14   Total Problems: Total Correct: Score: © Carson-Dellosa CD-2204

Name _____   Finding the Main Idea

Read each passage and question. Circle the letter beside the correct answer.

Clouds

Clouds look like giant balls of cotton, but they are not made of cotton at all. Rather, clouds are formations in the Earth's atmosphere that consist mainly of water. A part of the water cycle, clouds are accumulations of water that have evaporated from the Earth's surface and collected in a large area high above the earth. The evaporated water becomes vapor and expands and cools as it rises into the air. Since air can only hold a certain amount of water, the vapor can change to water again if the air gets cooler. This becomes rain on Earth. If the temperature is cold enough, the water vapor changes to ice rather than to water, thus ice or snow is produced. Clouds can tell us a lot about the temperature, the moisture in the air, and the potential for a storm.

1. What is the main idea of this paragraph?
   A. Clouds are little weather stations.
   B. Clouds usually help in predicting the weather.
   (C) how clouds are formed
   D. where clouds usually are in the atmosphere

Learning to Read

Learning to read is something that is usually done in the early grades. Everyone can benefit in many ways from knowing how to read. Putting sounds with letters and then combining letters and sounds to make words is the basic level of learning to read. As the reading process continues, it is imperative to practice all the reading skills. Reading then becomes the main tool for getting information on practically any topic. Being able to read is a huge factor in one's success—both academically and professionally. It enables a person to be knowledgable in an ever changing world.

2. The main idea of this paragraph is:
   A. It is tough to learn how to read.
   (B) Reading is fundamental to many other things.
   C. Reading can be difficult at times.
   D. Most children can read before they enter kindergarten.

© Carson-Dellosa CD-2204   Total Problems: Total Correct: Score: **15**

Name _____   Finding Facts

Read the passage and place a check in the blank next to each statement that is a fact from the paragraph.

Abraham Lincoln

Abraham Lincoln was the sixteenth president of the United States of America. He was a lawyer before becoming president and had a reputation for being extremely honest. Many of his political accomplishments include helping other people overcome adversity. These deeds certainly support how dedicated Mr. Lincoln was to the people of his country. Mr. Lincoln is known for his efforts to abolish slavery. He was dissatisfied with the injustices of slavery and was quick to see other people being oppressed or mistreated. The north and south did not agree for many years on the topic of slavery, but after years of civil war, slavery was abolished in the United States.

1. __✔__ Mr. Lincoln was known as an honest man.

2. _____ The ending of slavery is not considered an accomplishment of Lincoln's.

3. __✔__ Mr. Lincoln was the sixteenth president of the United States.

4. _____ Before becoming president, Mr. Lincoln did not have a career.

5. __✔__ Mr. Lincoln was committed to helping people in hardships.

16   Total Problems: Total Correct: Score: © Carson-Dellosa CD-2204

Finding Facts

Name _____

Read the passage and place a check in the blank next to each statement that is a fact from the paragraph.

Learning from Playing

Children learn from playing. It may sound strange, but it is true. Playing with toys can help babies learn about their environment. They can also learn that they are doing things themselves that cause certain events to happen. They begin to notice that a toy moves if they push it, a button may squeak if pressed, and a ball rolls when nudged. Learning to do new things is often a bridge of experience the child has had with an earlier situation. Remembering one event and relating it to another is an elaborate form of learning called reasoning.

Helping children play with a variety of toys is a wonderful way to foster early learning. It is important, however, to remember that all objects are not toys. Parents and child care workers should be very careful when selecting toys to give young children.

1. ✔ Children can learn from playing with toys.
2. _____ All toys either squeak or roll.
3. _____ A toy is any object that is fun to hold.
4. ✔ Children, at a relatively early age, understand they can do things to objects.
5. ✔ Parents should make careful toy purchases for their children.
6. ✔ Reasoning is when an old experience is related to a newer one.
7. _____ Usually, small children do not enjoy playing with balls or stuffed animals.

© Carson-Dellosa CD-2204   Total Problems: Total Correct: Score: **17**

Figurative Language

Name _____

Read each passage and question. Circle the letter beside the correct answer.

Paul and Wade

Paul and Wade are best friends. Paul is very messy and Wade is very neat and organized. Many times Wade has offered to help Paul become better organized. One day Paul misplaced a very important letter. It was his birthday letter from his grandmother. It had a twenty-dollar bill inside, too. He was very upset about losing the letter and he went to Wade to tell him that it was time to turn over a new leaf. He asked Wade for some help in getting everything in his bedroom organized. The two boys got busy with their work and after a few hours the room looked great. Paul even found the missing letter underneath a stack of papers on his desk.

1. What is meant in the paragraph by the phrase, "turn over a new leaf"?
   A. He should do more yard work each day for his father.
   (B) He should make a change for the better.
   C. He should plant trees so there will be more leaves in the environment.
   D. He should try something new whenever possible.

The Birdhouse

Donna and Mary had been working on their masterpiece birdhouse for the Garden Club show. They were getting very frustrated with the wire base they had created. It did not seem to be strong enough to hold the sides of the house up. There must be some way to make a base strong enough to support the rest of the structure. Donna had made a large frame with plenty of room inside for the birds. She had also measured the sections accurately and had just enough material to cover the entire birdhouse. After some discussion, Mary and Donna decided that not all of their design was bad. It was just necessary to remake the base. There was no need to throw the baby out with the bath water. A few changes would make the birdhouse into just what they designed. Donna went inside to find her father for help. He could make a wooden base. Mr. Johnson gladly came to help the girls and soon they were on their way to a splendid birdhouse for the show.

2. What is meant by the phrase "no need to throw the baby out with the bath water"?
   (A) Just because one part of a big project is not good, does not mean the entire thing is bad.
   B. Everyone has had a bad day before and if one thing goes wrong, that is not too bad.
   C. Everyone should be more patient when bathing children so that they are not accidentally hurt.
   D. Most people like to work on a project for a long time and get through their mistakes.

18   Total Problems: Total Correct: Score: © Carson-Dellosa CD-2204

Figurative Language

Name _____

Read each passage and question. Circle the letter beside the correct answer.

Shawn and Jason's Fort

Shawn liked to go exploring in the woods behind his house. On Saturday, his friend Jason came over to play with him. The two boys decided to go to the woodsy area and look for fallen tree limbs and things to use for a fort. They had been planning all winter to build a fort when the weather warmed up. Shawn knew exactly where to begin looking and the two boys were on their mission. Jason soon found a large tree limb and tried to pull it up from underneath some other brush. He pulled and pulled but never was able to make it budge. He yelled for Shawn to come help him. Shawn came over and Jason told him that the tree limb would be great, but it must weigh a ton. The two boys pulled and pulled but never succeeded in getting the limb.

1. What is meant by the phrase "it must weigh a ton"?
   A. An object is over 2,000 pounds according to standard measurement.
   (B) The object is extremely heavy.
   C. Sometimes trees get heavier as they become older and their branches fall.
   D. Every tree is extremely heavy.

Beth and Meg's Brownies

Beth and Meg were in the kitchen making their famous brownies. Well, at least they thought they were famous. The girls were best friends and they loved doing things together, especially cooking. They had been in the kitchen for only a few minutes when Meg accidentally dropped the entire bowl of brownie mix. It landed on the floor with a thud. The girls looked at the mess in total disbelief. Their day of brownie making was ruined. Beth's mother heard the noise and came into the kitchen to see what was going on. The girls looked so disappointed and quietly explained the accident. Beth's mother smiled and said that before they knew it gray skies would clear up. She helped the girls clean up the mess and then began a second batch of brownies.

2. What did Beth's mother mean by "gray skies would clear up"?
   A. When making a recipe there should not be more than two people helping.
   B. Sometimes, if too many people help do a job, it is not very helpful.
   C. Usually, people need help only if they ask someone for it.
   (D) Bad events will soon pass and good things will come.

© Carson-Dellosa CD-2204   Total Problems: Total Correct: Score: **19**

Drawing Conclusions

Name _____

Read each passage and question. Circle the letter beside the correct answer.

Taylor's Afternoon at Mom's Office

Every Wednesday Taylor liked going to her mother's office after school. Soon after Taylor arrived, there would be about ten cars arriving with dogs inside. Taylor would watch each owner park his or her car, get out and open the door for his or her precious pooch. All the dogs and the owners would gather in a clear area of the parking lot, in a circle. Soon, a lady would arrive and walk to the center of the circle. After giving a few directions, the crowd of dogs and people would begin to walk in an orderly fashion around and around the circle. Taylor loved watching this and she would beg her mother to wait a few more minutes before leaving so she could see the dogs a little longer.

1. Most likely, what is the scene Taylor is watching?
   A. A pet store is taking all of the dogs out for a chance to exercise.
   (B) A dog obedience class is starting.
   C. It is a pet adoption day at a nearby animal hospital.
   D. The local police station is training dogs to help in police work.

Mark and Amy

Mark and Amy entered the building and quickly got in line to buy their tickets. After they each had a ticket, they passed through another door, giving the man at the door their tickets. He tore the tickets in half and return a stub to them to keep. Mark saw a few friends he recognized and went over to speak while Amy got in line for popcorn and sodas. Soon the two friends walked down a carpeted hallway and entered a large, dark room. They selected two seats near the back of the room and began munching on their snacks. Soon the screen before them lit up, and loud music began to play.

2. Most likely, where are Mark and Amy?
   (A) at a movie theater
   B. at a restaurant
   C. at a shopping mall
   D. at a football game

20   Total Problems: Total Correct: Score: © Carson-Dellosa CD-2204

Name _____ Drawing Conclusions

Read each passage and question. Circle the letter beside the correct answer.

Nancy and Sonya

Nancy and Sonya were so nervous about their performances. They only had to wait now. What were the judges going to decide? The girls were giddy with anxious anticipation. Nancy and Sonya knew they had practiced and had memorized all the cheers perfectly. Certainly they would make the squad. They had been taking gymnastics for seven years! Their jumps and flips were almost perfect. The girls felt like the time was just crawling by. Hopefully the results would be good and the girls would have another dream come true! They were so excited about possibly being on the sidelines of the football games next season!

1. Most likely, what were the girls doing?
   A. taking lessons on how to be cheerleaders
   B. trying out for the cheerleading squad
   C. trying to be on the school gymnastic team
   D. trying to see who had a better jump than the other one

Lee and Dad

Lee and his dad were packing their things in the car. They had a cooler with plenty of drinks and snacks. They also had on their baseball caps. Once the sports-crazy-duo drove away, they began chatting about the plans for the day. Lee asked his father several times about the tickets and his father assured him they were in his pocket. In minutes, the stadium was in sight. Lee could hardly stay calm. He grabbed a few drinks and snacks from the cooler and stuffed them into his backpack. They parked the car and headed for the huge black gates. Once inside, Lee noticed a sign that pointed to an area where kids could run the bases before the game. Mr. Wilson agreed to let his son participate while he watched. Lee soon came back to his dad and the two headed off to find their seats for the day.

2. Most likely, what are Lee and his father doing?
   A. going to baseball practice
   B. going to the batting cages
   C. going to a baseball game
   D. going to baseball summer camp

© Carson-Dellosa CD-2204

| Total Problems: | Total Correct: | Score: |

21

Name _____ Monica's Journal

Read the journal entries and answer the questions on the following page.

<u>Monday, December 7</u>

Sara told Jenny today that she was going to start taking ice-skating lessons. I started taking lessons only a week ago and now my whole fifth-grade class is going to copy me! I think there are other things people could do for fun and exercise. Oh well, mom says it is flattering when others do things like you. I don't see that. I like ice-skating because that is something I can do without my little brother! I know mom needs a lot of help with him, but he really can take up a lot of my time.

<u>Tuesday, December 8</u>

I hope I did okay on my science test today! That class really can be hard sometimes. I really like Mrs. Johnson for a teacher. She explains things really well. Plus the experiments she lets us do are so much fun. Surely, I made an "A" on that test. I hope so, anyway!

<u>Wednesday, December 9</u>

My dad returns from his business trip on Thursday. I can't wait. He promised to pick me up from school and take me to get an ice cream, a new pair of jeans, and a necklace. Shopping with Dad is a lot of fun. I think it is because he doesn't really remember what I already have at home. So, we don't fuss about clothes like mom and I do.

<u>Thursday, December 10</u>

Wow, I cannot believe it is already about to be Christmas! This year has gone by so quickly! I hope we get to go to my grandmother's this year for Christmas. She is retired and has all this time to do stuff for my little brother and me. She is a great cook! She makes great cookies and cakes, and her turkey and stuffing are fantastic!

22

© Carson-Dellosa CD-2204

Name _____ Monica's Journal

Read each question and circle the letter beside the correct answer.

1. Monica's father would be returning soon from:
   A. a ball game
   B. work
   C. a business trip
   D. a movie

2. What grade is Monica in at school?
   A. 4th
   B. 3rd
   C. 5th
   D. 6th

3. Why does Monica feel that Sara and Jenny are "copying" her?
   A. Because they wear the same kinds of clothes as Monica.
   B. Because they are beginning to take ice-skating lessons.
   C. Because they are in her class and watch her all of the time.
   D. Because they are trying to talk like her.

4. What does Monica like about her science teacher?
   A. She likes the tests because they are usually hard.
   B. She likes it when the teacher lets the class go outside.
   C. She likes the experiments and the way she explains things.
   D. She likes the cool clothes her teacher wears to class.

5. What does Monica like about visiting her grandmother?
   A. She likes to play with her dog and cats.
   B. She likes to help her grandmother work in the flower beds.
   C. She likes when her grandmother tells funny stories to her.
   D. She likes her grandmother's cooking.

6. With whom does Monica enjoy shopping?
   A. her dad
   B. her mom
   C. Jenny
   D. Sara

© Carson-Dellosa CD-2204

| Total Problems: | Total Correct: | Score: |

23

Name _____ Scott's Journal

Read the journal entries and answer the questions on the following page.

<u>Tuesday, November 5</u>

I don't know why, but for some reason I have decided to start writing a journal. My teacher said that it can be a fun thing to do. She even said that people just write about their thoughts in a journal so it doesn't have to be fancy or for anyone else to read. I like that. I think I'll do this for a few weeks to see how it goes.

<u>Wednesday, November 6</u>

Well, today is day two of my journal. I had a pretty good day at school. I think my friend Brent is crazy though. He said he liked our substitute teacher in math today. We usually have Mrs. Anderson and today she was sick so we had a sub. Her name was Mrs. Jenkins. I thought she looked funny, but Brent said she explained division to him very well. I prefer waiting to talk to Mrs. Anderson when she gets back. Well, that's all I can write today. I have to go to football practice now.

<u>Thursday, November 7</u>

I am so tired today! I think our coach expects us to be like professional football players or something. We had a hard practice yesterday. We certainly should win our game tomorrow afternoon. Well, I have to do my homework now. I'll write more tomorrow.

<u>Friday, November 8</u>

I have really surprised myself about writing in my journal. I even think about it at school and I plan some things to write when I get home. Like today, I had a great time at football practice and my friend José is going to come over to my house on Saturday. I like hanging around with him. I don't think I will tell him about my journal though, since it's kind of private. I don't want to tell anyone really. Maybe I will tell my mom, but that's all. And speaking of Mom, I hear her calling for me. Until tomorrow!

24

© Carson-Dellosa CD-2204

Name _____   Scott's Journal

Read each question and circle the letter beside the correct answer.

1. Who is the writer's friend?
   A. Brent
   B. Scott
   C. Mrs. Anderson
   D. Mrs. Jenkins

2. What event takes place for Scott on Wednesday?
   A. football practice
   B. a parade
   C. a football game
   D. a birthday party

3. What does Brent like about Mrs. Jenkins?
   A. She's a good artist.
   B. She likes football.
   C. She explains division well.
   D. She tells funny jokes

4. When is Scott's game?
   A. Tuesday
   B. Wednesday
   C. Thursday
   D. Friday

5. What caused Scott to stop writing in his journal on Friday?
   A. His friend Jose came over to his house.
   B. His mom was calling for him.
   C. His sister came into his room.
   D. He was tired of keeping a journal.

Total Problems: _____ Total Correct: _____ Score: _____   **25**

Name _____   A Lady

Read the poem and each question that follows. Circle the letter beside the correct answer.

A Lady

A lady wore a hat to the town's parade.
It had a big, red flower perched on top.
I saw her somewhere later, drinking lemonade;
I guess she prefers that drink to plain old soda pop.

She did look peculiar in her flower hat;
I'd never, ever seen anything like that before.
She also had a bag in which she carried her cat.
But, I heard she's really nice, and knows my best friend Matt!

Then, just two days later I saw her wear a sock.
I think it was pink and orange with big red polka dots.
She looked a little funny, but it wasn't quite a shock,
'Cause it seems she just likes dressing and visiting town a lots.

1. What is the meaning of the poem?
   A. A lady is trying to dress for going downtown.
   B. A bystander notices a lady who is unusual.
   C. A parade usually has a variety of odd people.
   D. A town has different people who like different things.

2. When did the author first notice the lady?
   A. at the restaurant   B. at the parade
   C. at a store   D. at a party

3. What was the lady wearing on her hat?
   A. a blue butterfly   B. a purple dot
   C. a red flower   D. a button

4. What was the lady carrying in her bag?
   A. a cat   B. a sandwich
   C. a bird   D. a dog

5. What had polka dots?
   A. the lady's sock   B. the lady's bag
   C. a bird's cage   D. a box

26   Total Problems: _____ Total Correct: _____ Score: _____

Name _____   My Rainbow

Read the poem and each question that follows. Circle the letter beside the correct answer.

My Rainbow

I wished for a rainbow to span through the sky.
Bystanders would notice as it catches the eye.

The colors to be vivid and easy to see,
I'd walk through the city with it following me.

Tall buildings may stretch to amazing heights,
But leave my rainbow in perfect sight.

I'd really be lucky to have such a treasure,
Which would also bring others moments of pleasure.

My rainbow and me, a wonderful pair,
My wish, my hope, for sometime out there.

1. What was the person in the poem hoping for?
   A. rain   B. sunshine   C. a rainbow   D. tall buildings

2. Where did the person imagine seeing the rainbow?
   A. in a grassy field   B. over a pond
   C. in a desert   D. in a city

3. Why does the person seem to think that the rainbow is following him or her?
   A. Because it continues to be visible in the city among all of the buildings.
   B. Because it is moving through the sky with the force of the wind.
   C. Because he or she is in a car and the rainbow seems to be moving.
   D. Because most rainbows move around in the sky.

4. What human ability did the writer say the buildings seem to have?
   A. lying down   B. stretching   C. running   D. sitting

5. According to the poem, why does the person want a rainbow?
   A. Because he or she doesn't have very many friends.
   B. Because he or she really likes rainbows and feels they bring happiness.
   C. Because he or she has never seen one before.
   D. Because he or she thinks they look funny in the sky.

Total Problems: _____ Total Correct: _____ Score: _____   **27**

Name _____   My Walk

Read the poem and each question that follows. Circle the letter beside the correct answer.

My Walk

I walked home from school the other day,
And took a different, more scenic, way.

A small red bird was eating some bread.
As he nibbled, I noticed him bobbing his head.

When I walked on further down my new path,
I saw this squirrel giving his tail a bath.

He didn't even notice that I stopped to look,
Nor did the old man who was reading his book.

The park is a neat and wonderful place.
It gives me a smile right on my face.

1. Where was the person when he or she saw the bird?
   A. at school   B. at home
   C. at the park   D. in the city

2. Why did the person go home a different way?
   A. It was a faster way home.
   B. It was a more scenic way.
   C. It was raining and this way was easier.
   D. He or she wanted to meet a friend.

3. Why did the person stop to watch things in the park?
   A. He or she found them interesting.
   B. It was part of a homework assignment.
   C. The old man told him or her to watch those things.
   D. He or she will never see a bird like that again.

4. What does the author mean by the word "bobbing"?
   A. moving from side to side
   B. moving in circles
   C. moving up and down
   D. making very still

28   Total Problems: _____ Total Correct: _____ Score: _____

One Big Cat

Name _____   One Big Cat

Read the passage and answer the questions that follow.

One Big Cat

Graceful, alert, and cunning, leopards are the third largest animal of the cat family. They live mostly in Africa and Asia. Only the lion and tiger are larger cats than the leopard. A large male can weigh up to one hundred sixty pounds. A big female may weigh up to eighty pounds.

Leopards are usually light tan with many black spots close together. Leopards are fierce animals who usually eat meat. They hunt their prey and rarely attack humans. These animals are unbelievably strong and can lift other animals very close to their own size. They are excellent climbers and often hide in trees to eat or watch for approaching prey.

While leopards are naturally wild, some have been captured and taught to be somewhat gentle. However, they are never suitable house pets. Their instincts are to hunt and kill their food. They are ferocious animals that belong in the wild.

1. What animals in the cat family are larger than the leopard? _lion and tiger_

2. Where do leopards often hide to capture their prey? _in trees_

3. Why are leopards not suitable house pets? _they are ferocious and wild_

4. On what continents are leopard populations usually found? _Africa and Asia_

5. What do leopards look like? _light tan with black spots_

Total Problems: Total Correct: Score: **29**

© Carson-Dellosa CD-2204

Name _____   Scotland

Read the passage and answer the questions that follow.

Scotland

Scotland is one of four countries that make up the United Kingdom of Great Britain and Northern Ireland. Scotland is a constitutional monarchy and Queen Elizabeth II is the head of state. The two largest cities in Scotland are Glasgow and Edinburgh. Edinburgh is the capital although it is smaller than Glasgow.

English is the country's dominant language and people are known for their closely knit families. The Scots refer to their larger family as a clan. Each clan often has a tartan plaid fabric they use to identify themselves. This tartan is commonly made into a formal clothing article called a kilt.

The economy of Scotland is supported by trade and manufacturing. The coastal ports allow ample opportunities for Scotland to import and export goods. Much of Scotland's food is imported while manufactured products are major exports.

Scotland is a beautiful country famous for its mountainous terrain, known as the highlands. Many tourists visit Scotland for its beauty, history, and leisure activities. The game of golf was invented in Scotland in the 1100s and remains popular there today. Other favorite sports of the Scots include association football—or soccer, hiking, mountain climbing, and fishing. The Highland Games take place each year and include events such as track, dance, tossing the caber, bagpipe playing and others.

1. What is the capital of Scotland? _Edinburgh_

2. What term is used by Scottish people that means "family"? _clan_

3. What sport was invented in Scotland? _golf_

4. How could the land in Scotland be described? _mountainous_

5. Who is the head of state for Scotland? _Queen Elizabeth II_

30   Total Problems: Total Correct: Score:

© Carson-Dellosa CD-2204

Name _____   Scotland

Refer to the passage on page 30 to solve this puzzle.

Scotland Crossword Puzzle

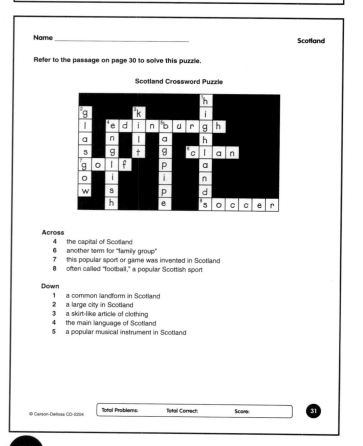

Across
4 the capital of Scotland
6 another term for "family group"
7 this popular sport or game was invented in Scotland
8 often called "football," a popular Scottish sport

Down
1 a common landform in Scotland
2 a large city in Scotland
3 a skirt-like article of clothing
4 the main language of Scotland
5 a popular musical instrument in Scotland

© Carson-Dellosa CD-2204   Total Problems: Total Correct: Score: **31**

Name _____   Robert Browning

Read the passage and answer the questions on the following page.

Robert Browning

Robert Browning was born in May of 1812 in London. His wealthy parents were able to provide lots of books for him to read. His father, a banker, encouraged him to learn all about the arts and literature. He attended school rather irregularly, but did eventually enter college. He did not ever complete his education, instead he began to publish many of his poems. Browning is best known for his romantic monologue poetry. He received some criticism for his first published poem as it took a deep look into very personal things in his life. Browning felt this was too harsh and had a difficult time overcoming the remarks. After that, he wrote in a way that exemplified his ability to seem emotional, but the emotions were not from personal experiences.

Writing was the way Robert Browning found he could communicate his thoughts and feelings. This became reality as he courted the lovely Elizabeth Barrett, who was also a poet. Miss Barrett lived with her father because she was in poor health and unable to live alone. She was able to move only in a wheelchair. She had written to Browning about his poetry that interested her and soon the letter writing turned into a romantic courtship.

Their relationship developed so far that Browning took Elizabeth on a trip and they were secretly married. Elizabeth's doctors felt her health would improve if she moved to Italy. When she married Mr. Browning, he immediately took her to Italy where she received excellent care.

As Mr. Browning's work did not provide him with a large salary, he and his wife lived on a very small income for a long time. One day a cousin of Elizabeth's from London began sending her one hundred pounds a week. Just before he died, he willed her a total of eleven thousand pounds. The couple did not have to worry about money after that. They remained in Italy and visited France and England on vacations. Today many modern poets continue to study the works of Robert Browning. He influenced many with his incredible talent for romantic monologue. This was by far his greatest accomplishment and contribution to poetry. His plays were not as popular as his poetry, yet he did receive recognition for a variety of writings.

32   © Carson-Dellosa CD-2204

© Carson-Dellosa CD-2204

Name _____

Robert Browning

Read each question. Circle the letter beside the correct answer.

1. What country is Robert Browning from originally?
   A. Ireland
   (B) England
   C. United States
   D. Italy

2. How did he and Elizabeth Barrett meet each other?
   A. telephone calls
   B. at school
   (C) through letters
   D. in the hospital

3. Where did Elizabeth live when she was writing to Mr. Browning?
   (A) with her father
   B. with her cousin
   C. with her sister
   D. with her neighbor

4. What did Robert and Elizabeth do secretly?
   A. write poetry
   (B) get married
   C. move to Italy
   D. teach her to walk

5. Why did they move to Italy?
   (A) for better health
   B. for better jobs
   C. for more money
   D. to help others

6. How did the couple get money for living expenses?
   A. They received money from her father and insurance.
   B. They received money from his writing and hers.
   (C) They were paid for his work and received money from a will.
   D. They performed plays and taught poetry at local colleges.

7. What is Robert Browning's greatest literary contribution?
   (A) writing poems with a romantic monologue
   B. writing plays with sad endings
   C. helping his wife improve her health
   D. writing letters to people to cheer them up

© Carson-Dellosa CD-2204 | Total Problems: ___ Total Correct: ___ Score: ___ | **33**

Name _____

Robert Browning

Refer to the passage on page 32 to solve this puzzle.

Robert Browning Crossword Puzzle

Across
3. the month of Robert Browning's birth
5. a kind of relative—Elizabeth was sent money from hers
6. wife of Robert Browning
8. a way of communicating through the mail
9. the type of writing Browning is famous for

Down
1. having to do with one's feelings
2. place of Mr. Browning's birth
4. his father's occupation
7. A doctor suggested Elizabeth move to this country.

34 | Total Problems: ___ Total Correct: ___ Score: ___ | © Carson-Dellosa CD-2204

Name _____

Sir Edmund Hillary

Read the passage and answer the questions on the following page.

Sir Edmund Hillary

Sir Edmund Hillary was the first person to climb Mt. Everest in the Himalayas. Mt. Everest stands over twenty-nine thousand feet tall and is five and one half miles above sea level. Sir Edmund completed his climb on May 29, 1953. Since then, there have been many expeditions to reach the summit. Many have had success, but some climbers have fallen victim to the dangers along the way, such as steep slopes, extreme cold, thin air, and avalanches.

Mt. Everest is located north of India in the Himalayan range. Many surveyors and climbers in nearby Tibet and Nepal have been attracted to the mountain's challenging landscape. Climbing the south side of the mountain is most common. Some have attempted to climb the west ridge, which is more difficult. Still today there are exuberant mountain climbers and thrill seeking individuals who will attempt the feat of reaching the summit of the tallest mountain in the world—Mt. Everest.

© Carson-Dellosa CD-2204 | **35**

Name _____

Sir Edmund Hillary

Read each statement and decide if it is true or false. Place a T or F in the blank next to the statement.

1. __T__ Sir Edmund Hillary was the first to climb Mt. Everest.
2. __T__ Mt. Everest is 5½ miles above sea level.
3. __T__ The Himalayas are located north of India.
4. __F__ Cold temperatures, strong winds, and steep slopes help climbers reach the top easily.
5. __T__ The summit is the highest point of a mountain.

Reader's Response: Write why you think some people enjoy mountain climbing.

(answers may vary)

_____
_____
_____
_____
_____
_____
_____
_____
_____
_____
_____
_____
_____

36 | Total Problems: ___ Total Correct: ___ Score: ___ | © Carson-Dellosa CD-2204

Name _____   Sir Edmund Hillary

Refer to the passage on page 35 to solve this puzzle.

Sir Edmund Hillary Crossword Puzzle

Across

5 word often used to describe a mountain climbing trip
6 flexible heavy cord used for tying and pulling
7 a large mass of snow or ice moving swiftly down a mountainside
9 a very straight and high incline

Down

1 the very top of the mountain
2 not straight; an incline
3 a very large hill, great for climbing
4 a high overhanging face of rock
5 the tallest mountain in the world
8 to move up a mountain

© Carson-Dellosa CD-2204 | Total Problems: | Total Correct: | Score: | **37**

Name _____   Critters Called Clams

Read the passage and answer the questions on the following page.

Critters Called Clams

What has one foot and sprays water at its enemies? Well, it's a clam. You may be fortunate enough one day to actually find a live clam in its shell on the beach. However, the clam notices danger very quickly and will pull its one foot inside its shell and just lie there. You can try as hard as you can to open the shell with your hands, but it won't open. The clam's soft body lives in the shell and it travels on land with the one foot it has. When danger seems to be near, the clam can spray water toward the area of danger. This is its way of protecting itself.

Sea gulls like to eat clams. Many times you may find empty clam shells on the shore. Those clams were probably eaten by a sea gull. Often times the clam can even escape from the sea gull's watchful eye. If a clam senses danger and the predator does not leave after being sprayed with water, the clam can bury itself in the sand and all you may see is a bubble in the sand. This is often hard to see and many times clams remain safe from hunters that way.

Clam digging is the way most fishermen harvest their clams. Just at the edge of the surf on the beach, one can dig up the sand and often find clams hidden. They are attempting to hide until they choose to go back out to sea. In restaurants clams are a popular seafood item and are often served steamed in their shells.

38   © Carson-Dellosa CD-2204

Name _____   Critters Called Clams

Read each question and write your answer in the space provided.

1. How does the clam travel on shore? _with its one foot_____

2. What does the clam do when danger seems near? _spray water toward the_
   _danger area_____

3. Who enjoys eating clams? _sea gulls and people_____

4. How can fishermen gather clams? _by digging into the sand- just at the_
   _edge of the surf_____

5. What is the clam's body like? _it is soft_____

6. Where do clams often hide? _in the sand_____

7. Why are clam shells often found on shore with no clams inside? _they have been_
   _eaten by sea gulls_____

8. How can someone tell if a clam is hidden in the sand? _there will be a small_
   _bubble in the sand_____

© Carson-Dellosa CD-2204 | Total Problems: | Total Correct: | Score: | **39**

Name _____   Great Ball of Fire

Read the passage and the statements that follow. Decide if each statement is true or false. Place a T or F in the blank next to each statement.

Great Ball of Fire

The sun is over ninety million miles from Earth. Measuring over one hundred times the Earth's diameter, the sun is a huge ball of gasses glowing at the center of the solar system. The sun is the closest star to Earth.

While the size seems to be enormous, it is important to remember that without the sun, human beings could not live. The heat and light provided by the sun sustains life for every plant and animal on earth.

Temperatures on Earth are greatly affected by the sun. When the sun's light hits the Earth at a direct angle, that area experiences a warm or hot season. When the sun's light hits the Earth at an indirect angle, that area experiences a cool or cold season.

Scientists have studied the sun for many years. They have discovered many things about the sun that have helped humanity. They predict the sun will continue to be a source of energy for another five billion years.

1. _T_ The sun is a star.

2. _T_ The sun sustains life on earth.

3. _F_ The sun is in another solar system near us.

4. _T_ The angle of sunlight affects temperatures on earth.

5. _F_ The sun will no longer exist in five million years.

6. _T_ People use the sun for heat and light.

40 | Total Problems: | Total Correct: | Score: | © Carson-Dellosa CD-2204

Name _____ Great Ball of Fire

Refer to the passage on page 40 to solve this puzzle.

Great Ball of Fire Crossword Puzzle

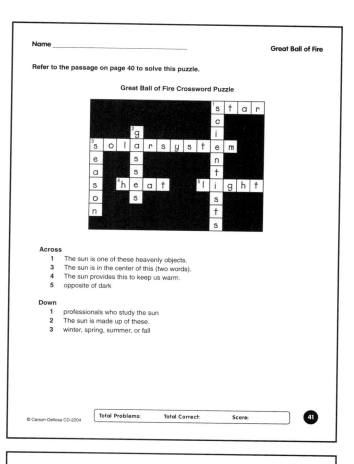

Across
1. The sun is one of these heavenly objects.
3. The sun is in the center of this (two words).
4. The sun provides this to keep us warm.
5. opposite of dark

Down
1. professionals who study the sun
2. The sun is made up of these.
3. winter, spring, summer, or fall

© Carson-Dellosa CD-2204   Total Problems: Total Correct: Score: **41**

Name _____ Something Sweet

Read the passage and the questions that follow. Circle the letter beside the correct answer.

Something Sweet

Whether it is from sugar cane or sugar beets, it may wind up in a sugar bowl one day. Sugar is a popular and tasty food and the United States is a leading producer of raw sugar.

Raw sugar is obtained through a process that purifies the plant into syrup, then dehydrates the liquid so crystals will form. Though some crystals form in the liquid, the liquid is still suitable for use in some foods. When the crystals are removed, raw sucrose remains.

In order for this liquid to be made into white table sugar, more steps are involved. The liquid's molasses film is removed, the crystals are dissolved in water, and then filtered and evaporated. A final step involves spinning the filtered liquid at a very high speed which causes crystals to form. When dried, the crystals become the white granules that we use at home.

Sugar products and refined sugar have been around for many years. However, the process of refining sugar has become more efficient and widespread with the help of technology. So, the next time you eat a piece of candy or taste a slice of pie, remember that sweet taste is most likely from the special ingredient called sugar.

1. Raw sugar is made from:
   A. sugar beets
   B. sugar cane
   C. molasses
   (D) both A and B

2. The United States is a leading producer of:
   A. sugar cane
   (B) raw sugar
   C. refined sugar
   D. molasses

3. Making white table sugar basically involves:
   (A) film removed, crystals dissolved, evaporation, spinning
   B. crystals added, film removed, water added
   C. evaporation, crystals dissolved, filtered
   D. filtering, molasses added, granules removed

4. Some foods use a liquid form of sugar:
   (A) true
   B. false

42   Total Problems: Total Correct: Score: © Carson-Dellosa CD-2204

Name _____ Something Sweet

Refer to the passage on page 42 to solve this puzzle.

Something Sweet Crossword Puzzle

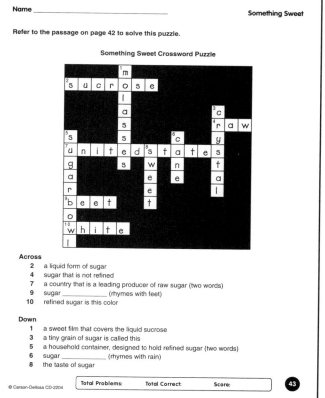

Across
2. a liquid form of sugar
4. sugar that is not refined
7. a country that is a leading producer of raw sugar (two words)
9. sugar _____ (rhymes with feet)
10. refined sugar is this color

Down
1. a sweet film that covers the liquid sucrose
3. a tiny grain of sugar is called this
5. a household container, designed to hold refined sugar (two words)
6. sugar _____ (rhymes with rain)
8. the taste of sugar

© Carson-Dellosa CD-2204   Total Problems: Total Correct: Score: **43**

Name _____ A Day at the Park

Read the passage and answer the questions on the following page.

A Day at the Park

Ted and James were playing ball at the park in their neighborhood when they heard a faint whimper in the distance. The boys continued their game of catch, and later took turns pitching to each other. They were certain that Coach Brown was going to be impressed with their improvement. As it was time for them to gather their things and go home, the boys walked to the large oak tree to retrieve their bikes. There, they heard the whimpering sound again. Puzzled, the two boys began looking to see from where the small sound might be coming.

Ted searched in one direction and James went in another. One more time the small sound made its presence. It was practically right under James. He bent down and began searching through the leaves and brush. To his surprise he uncovered a small, fluffy, gray kitten. He began talking softly to the kitten and assured him everything was going to be okay. The poor animal seemed terribly frightened.

James called for Ted to let him know he had discovered a kitten, and that's where the sound was coming from in the woods. Ted was surprised to see the tiny little animal so scared and alone. The boys decided to take the kitten home. Dr. Davis, Ted's father, was a veterinarian, so he would be able to tell if the little kitten was in good health. Ted put the kitten in his large pocket on the front of his coat and off they went.

They arrived at Ted's house and quickly found Dr. Davis. The boys told him all about the visit to the park and how they found the kitten. Dr. Davis took the little kitten and began looking it over very carefully. He seemed to think the kitten was in pretty good health. He was most likely hungry and thirsty. James filled a bowl with water and Ted got a can of cat food. The little kitten slowly began eating and drinking. After a few minutes, the kitten curled up into a gray ball and went to sleep.

James and Ted asked if they would be able to keep the kitten. Dr. Davis felt like that would be okay, but if they heard of a lost gray kitten, they would have to give him up. The boys understood and they stayed by the side of their new furry friend the rest of the day. The day of ball practice really took a different turn that day for Ted and James.

44   © Carson-Dellosa CD-2204

© Carson-Dellosa CD-2204

Name _____ A Day at the Park

Read each question. Circle the letter beside the correct answer.

1. What did James and Ted find at the park?
   A. a baseball
   B. a pile of leaves
   C. a boy
   (D) a kitten

2. What made the boys think there was something in the woods?
   A. They saw something move.
   (B) They heard a sound.
   C. Someone told them about it.
   D. They saw it wander into the woods.

3. How did the kitten get to Ted's house?
   (A) He rode in Ted's pocket.
   B. James carried him.
   C. Dr. Davis picked him up.
   D. Coach Brown let him ride in the car.

4. Who did the boys ask to examine the kitten?
   A. Mrs. Davis
   B. James's father
   (C) Ted's father
   D. Coach Brown

5. What did the kitten need?
   A. milk   B. a bath
   (C) food and water   D. its mother

6. What were the boys planning to do with the kitten?
   A. sell the kitten to a good home
   (B) keep it and take care of it
   C. give the kitten to Dr. Davis
   D. they didn't know

7. Why did the boys go to the park?
   A. They had a baseball game.
   B. They were looking for something Ted had lost.
   (C) They were practicing pitching and hitting.
   D. They were riding their bikes.

© Carson-Dellosa CD-2204 | Total Problems: | Total Correct: | Score: | **45**

Name _____ Two Girls Having Fun

Read the passage and the questions that follow. Circle the letter beside the correct answer.

Two Girls Having Fun

Most Saturday nights, Laura and Mei Li go to the theater to see a movie. The girls are best friends and have always enjoyed watching movies. Laura chooses the movie one week, and Mei Li will choose the next week's movie. The girls started their tradition while they were in the fourth grade. Now that they are in the fifth grade, they hope to continue it for as long as they can.

Usually Mei Li's mother, Mrs. Kim, takes the girls to the theater. While the girls are watching the movie, Mrs. Kim goes to the jewelry store next door, which is owned by her sister. Mrs. Kim waits for the girls at the store and uses the time to visit her sister. After the movie, the girls go to the jewelry store to find Mrs. Kim.

Laura and Mei Li love to pretend they are rich ladies shopping for diamonds when they go to the jewelry store. They often act silly and begin laughing at themselves. However, they never do it when the store is open since that would be distracting to real customers.

Laura and Mei Li have a special friendship and they hope to find even more fun things to do together in the future. But for now, it is fun being best friends and movie pals.

1. What do Laura and Mei Li do for fun?
   (A) watch movies and pretend to be rich ladies shopping
   B. pretend to be movie stars walking into a famous place
   C. make jewelry and wear expensive clothes
   D. look for hidden treasures

2. Where does Mrs. Kim's sister work?
   A. the movie theater
   (B) a jewelry store
   C. a grocery store
   D. a clothing store

3. When do the girls go to the movies?
   A. Fridays
   B. Thursdays
   C. Sundays
   (D) Saturdays

46 | Total Problems: | Total Correct: | Score: | © Carson-Dellosa CD-2204

Name _____ Two Girls Having Fun

Refer to the passage on page 46 to solve this puzzle.

Two Girls Having Fun Crossword Puzzle

Across
1 the grade Laura and Mei Li are in — fifth
3 the type of jewelry the girls pretend to shop for — diamonds
6 the name of the building where movies are shown — theater

Down
1 Mei Li and Laura are best _____ — friends
2 the type of store Mrs. Kim's sister owns — jewelry
4 the girls see one _____ most weeks — movie
5 most Saturday _____ the girls go to the movies — nights

© Carson-Dellosa CD-2204 | Total Problems: | Total Correct: | Score: | **47**

Name _____ Morris and Dave

Read the passage and answer the questions on the following page.

Morris and Dave

Dave was a normal twelve-year-old boy living in a small town who wanted fun things to do after school each day. He didn't have any brothers or sisters to play with like other kids. Dave didn't play on a sports team, take horseback riding lessons, or even have a hobby. Once his homework was done, he would either watch television or read a book. He was convinced his life was the most boring life any kid could have.

Dave's grandfather lived in the house next door. Sometimes Dave would go to his house and talk while his grandfather fed or brushed his horses. Dave loved his grandfather very much. He liked listening to his grandfather tell interesting stories. One day Dave went to his grandfather's farm and noticed a small dog was in the horse paddock running between the horse's legs. The horses did not seem bothered by the little dog, but occasionally they would kick their hind legs up to try to trip him. The horse's size did not seem to frighten the little guy at all. The dog was so quick that the movements and kicks of the horses were not hard for him to dodge.

Dave's grandfather explained that the little dog wandered up a few days ago. He figured the little dog was lost or had run away. Dave played with him for a while and begged his grandfather to let him keep the dog and care for him. His grandfather agreed and they became great friends.

The dog became known as Morris and he always kept the three horses—Timothy, Sally, and Duke—well entertained. From then on, every day after school Dave had something to which he looked forward. He could not wait to get off the bus and meet Morris in the field between the two houses. Dave was confident that he and Morris would be good friends for a very long time.

48 | © Carson-Dellosa CD-2204

Name _____

Morris and Dave

Read each question. Circle the letter beside the correct answer.

1. What did Dave usually do after school?
   - **A** watch TV
   - B. play football
   - C. go swimming
   - D. build things

2. Why did Dave like visiting his grandfather?
   - A. He liked helping care for the horses and the barn.
   - **B** He liked hearing his grandfather's stories.
   - C. He liked making things with his grandfather.
   - D. He liked working for his grandfather for extra money.

3. What did Dave find one day in the paddock?
   - A. a horse
   - B. a bird
   - **C** a dog
   - D. a cat

4. Where was Dave's house?
   - A. next to the school
   - B. near the train tracks
   - **C** next to his grandfather's
   - D. next to the library

5. What did Dave get that made him happy and no longer bored?
   - A. Daisy
   - B. Sally
   - C. Duke
   - **D** Morris

© Carson-Dellosa CD-2204

Total Problems: Total Correct: Score:

49

Name _____

The Town of Bakersville

Read the passage and answer the questions on the following page.

The Town of Bakersville

Mr. Leonard had worked for the fire department for many years. The people in the community were always happy to see Mr. Leonard in the big, red fire truck because they knew he was helping take care of the community. Bakersville was a small town with a big heart, people often said. People in this town really cared about one another.

One day, Mr. Leonard and his firemen were called to a fire. The call was about a small building that had caught fire from a nearby electrical pole. The building was a small pizza restaurant owned by a friend of Mr. Leonard's, Carl Jones. The fire truck raced to the little building and Mr. Leonard and his crew jumped off and began putting out the flames. Soon, the flames were out and the building was black from the burn. Fortunately, no one was inside.

Mr. Leonard stood in front of the building talking to Mr. Jones when suddenly they were both knocked over a distance of several feet and fell to the ground. Then a loud thud hit the ground and shook the earth. Stunned by the assault, the men looked up just in time to see Jason, Mr. Jones's son, standing over them. He pointed to where the men were standing and there was the burned electrical pole on the ground. The pole had fallen and the men didn't know it. Jason had shoved them out of the way just in time.

Gradually, the men gathered themselves and stood up to look at the accident. They thanked Jason for seeing the danger headed their way and helping them get out of its path. On the way to the fire truck, Mr. Leonard told Jason it was great to live in Bakersville where people are friendly enough to knock someone down whenever it is necessary. The men laughed and Mr. Leonard and his crew loaded up the truck and headed back to the station.

50

© Carson-Dellosa CD-2204

Name _____

The Town of Bakersville

Read each question. Circle the letter beside the correct answer.

1. What job did Mr. Leonard have?
   - A. policeman
   - **C** fireman
   - B. restaurant owner
   - D. banker

2. Where did the fire crew have to go to answer a call?
   - A. a store
   - **B** a restaurant
   - C. a house
   - D. a school

3. Why did Mr. Leonard get knocked down after the fire was out?
   - A. A tree fell on him.
   - **B** A boy pushed him.
   - C. A truck was going to hit him.
   - D. A dog was chasing him.

4. What caused the fire to start?
   - **A** an electrical pole
   - B. An oven was left turned on.
   - C. A candle was left burning.
   - D. a fire from another building

5. What were the townspeople's attitudes toward each other?
   - A. They were usually mean to each other for no reason.
   - **B** They were kind and cared for others.
   - C. They were always trying to start fires in town.
   - D. They were very private and didn't talk much to anyone.

6. Who was inside the burning building?
   - A. Mr. Jones
   - B. the crew
   - C. Jason
   - **D** no one

7. Why was it good for Mr. Jones to be knocked down by Jason?
   - A. He was in the way of the fire truck.
   - B. He was about to run into the burning building.
   - C. He was about to get wet.
   - **D** He was in the path of a falling pole.

© Carson-Dellosa CD-2204

Total Problems: Total Correct: Score:

51

Name _____

Melanie Plays Golf

Read the passage and answer the questions on the following page.

Melanie Plays Golf

One day Melanie's father came home from work with a long box in his arms. He called for her to come to the family room and see what he had. She came immediately and saw the box. "What's in the box?" she asked.

"Well, that's for you to find out. Here open it and see," replied her dad.

Melanie opened the box and pulled out a long, straight, silver stick. As she pulled it completely out she noticed that it was a golf club. Happily, Melanie took the club and began practicing her stance and a slow golf swing.

"Is this for me?" asked Melanie.

"Yes, it is. I noticed you had a really good time last week at the miniature golf course so I thought you might like to try a real golf course with me sometime," said her father.

"I'd like that a lot. I think if I practice I could be really good," she said.

"Sure you could," her father continued. "All it takes is a little skill and a lot of practice. Golf is a very interesting sport. Your mom and I would like to play more often."

"Hey, Dad," exclaimed Melanie, "Could we go play for a while this Saturday?"

"Yes, in fact I was already planning on it," he said.

"Great!" said Melanie, as she skipped out of the room, cheering.

52

© Carson-Dellosa CD-2204

© Carson-Dellosa CD-2204

89

Name _____ Melanie Plays Golf

Read each question. Circle the letter beside the correct answer.

1. Why was Melanie so excited?
   A. Her father had just come home from work.
   B. Her package had come in the mail.
   C. Her dad planned to take her to play golf.
   D. Her mom was giving her golf lessons.

2. Where was Melanie when she got her new club?
   A. at home
   B. at the miniature golf course
   C. at a party
   D. at school

3. When was the golf day going to be?
   A. Tuesday
   B. Friday
   C. Saturday
   D. Sunday

4. Who likes golf in Melanie's family?
   A. Mom and Dad
   B. only Dad
   C. Dad and Melanie
   D. Mom, Dad, and Melanie

5. How did Melanie feel about the surprise?
   A. very excited
   B. disappointed
   C. confused
   D. uncertain

6. For what occasion did Melanie get the surprise?
   A. no special occasion
   B. birthday
   C. end of school
   D. Valentine's Day

© Carson-Dellosa CD-2204 | Total Problems: | Total Correct: | Score: | **53**

Name _____ Turning Twelve

Read the passage and answer the questions on the following page.

Turning Twelve

Mark was turning twelve on Friday. He and his mom had planned his birthday party two weeks ago. He was having six fiends come home with him after school and spend the night. Jake, Joel, Frank, Matt, Chad, and Hugo were all coming to Mark's house. First, they would play in the backyard, and then they would have hot dogs and birthday cake. Mark was also very excited about getting to stay up as late as he and his friends wanted. It was going to be the best birthday ever!

As soon as the bus stopped at his house, the fun began. All seven boys jumped off the bus, went inside Mark's house, and put away their things. Mark's mother had popcorn and soda ready for snacks, and she even allowed them to watch a few cartoons while they ate. Soon the boys were in the backyard having fun.

After three hours of playing tag in the yard, telling jokes, and exploring Mark's new tree house, the group headed inside for dinner. Mark's dad grilled hot dogs for everyone. For dessert, there was, of course, cake and ice cream. Soon everyone was very full and getting tired. Mark opened his gifts and then suggested they watch a movie. Everyone was so exhausted. The movie had been on for only twenty-five minutes when all seven boys fell sound asleep.

The next morning the boys woke up and resumed their activities. First to the tree house, then to the garage for bikes, skateboards, and in-line skates. Mark's mom came out with a tray of hot muffins and juice for everyone for breakfast. Quickly, each one of them ate and, of course, continued playing. At eleven o'clock, several of the boys' mothers were arriving to pick them up. After everyone had gone, Mark thanked his mom for a wonderful birthday party. She smiled and said it was fun for her too. Mark admitted that the party was great fun, but the best thing is that he is now twelve years old.

54 © Carson-Dellosa CD-2204

Name _____ Turning Twelve

Read each question. Circle the letter beside the correct answer.

1. Who was having a birthday party?
   A. Frank
   B. Matt
   C. Mark
   D. Jake

2. Where did the boys play after school?
   A. in the house
   B. in the backyard
   C. in the garage
   D. in Mark's room

3. Who met the boys at home after school?
   A. Mark's mom
   B. Mark's dad
   C. Mark's grandmother
   D. Mark's best friend

4. What did the boys do after eating dinner?
   A. play in the backyard
   B. watch a movie
   C. do homework
   D. explore the neighborhood

5. What did the boys have to eat that night?
   A. popcorn
   B. pizza
   C. candy
   D. hot dogs

6. When did the boys begin going home the next day?
   A. 12 o'clock
   B. 10 o'clock
   C. 11 o'clock
   D. 1 o'clock

© Carson-Dellosa CD-2204 | Total Problems: | Total Correct: | Score: | **55**

Name _____ Turning Twelve

Refer to the passage on page 54 to solve this puzzle.

Turning Twelve Puzzle

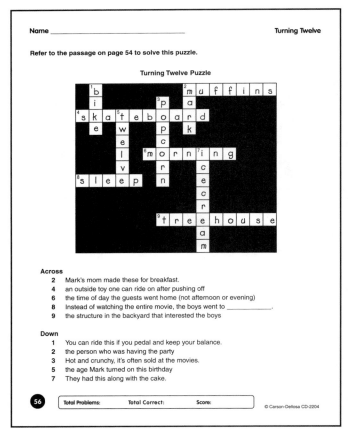

Across
2. Mark's mom made these for breakfast.
4. an outside toy one can ride on after pushing off
6. the time of day the guests went home (not afternoon or evening)
8. Instead of watching the entire movie, the boys went to _____.
9. the structure in the backyard that interested the boys

Down
1. You can ride this if you pedal and keep your balance.
2. the person who was having the party
3. Hot and crunchy, it's often sold at the movies.
5. the age Mark turned on this birthday
7. They had this along with the cake.

56 | Total Problems: | Total Correct: | Score: | © Carson-Dellosa CD-2204

The Happy Dragon

Name _____ The Happy Dragon

Read the passage and answer the questions that follow. Circle the letter beside the correct answer.

The Happy Dragon

Wendy Chen lives with her parents in the suburbs of a large city. Right before Wendy was born, her parents, Mr. and Mrs. Chen, moved to the United States from China. The Chens like America very much.

The Happy Dragon is the Chen's restaurant. Mr. and Mrs. Chen are both very good at making delicious Chinese foods. Mrs. Chen usually helps take care of the customers in the dining room, while Mr. Chen almost always works in the kitchen preparing food.

Wendy has been going to the restaurant with her parents all her life. She is now old enough to help at the restaurant. Each time customers sit down at a table, Wendy brings them ice water, hot tea, and fried noodles. Eventually, Wendy will take orders and be a waitress at the restaurant.

At school, Wendy's friends ask her lots of questions about the restaurant and Chinese food. Wendy likes to talk about the restaurant because she is proud of it and her parents. Many of her friends enjoy eating there with their families.

1. From where did the Chens immigrate?
   A. Norway
   B. Japan
   C. China
   D. Canada

2. What do Wendy's parents do for work?
   A. They own a restaurant.
   B. They are teachers.
   C. They build large houses.
   D. They have a movie theater.

3. How long has Wendy been going to the restaurant?
   A. about two years
   B. only three months
   C. all her life
   D. less than four years

4. When did Mr. and Mrs. Chen leave their native country?
   A. after Wendy was born
   B. before Wendy was born
   C. two years ago
   D. when they were little

© Carson-Dellosa CD-2204 | Total Problems: | Total Correct: | Score: | **57**

Name _____ Neil's Big Game

Read the passage and answer the questions on the following page.

Neil's Big Game

Neil went to bed exhausted after a very busy day. He had been to school, baseball practice, and a birthday party for his friend James. As soon as he crawled in bed, he immediately dropped off to sleep.

During the night, Neil began to dream. His mind took him to Dodger Stadium in May where the Major League baseball season was in full swing. Neil dreamed he was sitting on the bench in the dugout, right beside some of the biggest names in baseball. The game was in the third inning and the score was tied three to three.

Suddenly, the Dodgers' manager came over to Neil and told him he was in the lineup. Neil was shocked! He couldn't believe he was about to bat at Dodger Stadium. He took his place in the bull pen to warm up and began stretching and practicing his swing.

Minutes later he was at the plate. The first pitch came in low and fast. Neil swung and "crack"—his bat nailed the ball. It was a line drive to left field. Neil felt stuck for a second as he looked at what he had just done. A loud roar came from the Dodgers' dugout and off went Neil to first base.

The ball seemed to fly toward first base like a torpedo. Neil raced for the bag and his toes touched one second before the catch was made. He was safe! What a wonderful feeling! Neil happily let out a yell in celebration of his success.

Just then Neil opened his eyes. He was not in Dodger Stadium. He was lying in his bed! Wow, what a dream! Stunned by the reality the dream seemed to have, he sat up in his bed for a few minutes to savor the memory of being a Major League baseball player.

58 © Carson-Dellosa CD-2204

Name _____ Neil's Big Game

Read each question. Circle the letter beside the correct answer.

1. Why did Neil go to bed quickly?
   A. He was in trouble.
   B. He was very tired.
   C. He had to get up early the next day.
   D. It was getting late.

2. What did Neil do during the night?
   A. He fell out of the bed.
   B. His blanket came off.
   C. He had a dream.
   D. He snored very loudly.

3. What did Neil dream he was doing?
   A. He dreamed he was playing in a major league baseball game.
   B. He dreamed he was flying off a very high cliff.
   C. He dreamed he was sleeping in his bed.
   D. He dreamed he was falling from a cloud.

4. Where was Neil?
   A. at a baseball game
   B. at home in his bed
   C. at a carnival
   D. at school in his classroom

5. Why did Neil seem shocked when he heard a loud "crack."
   A. He was scared that a tree was falling on top of him.
   B. He was surprised that the weather was getting so bad.
   C. He was amazed that he hit the ball so far.
   D. He was upset because he broke his mother's vase.

© Carson-Dellosa CD-2204 | Total Problems: | Total Correct: | Score: | **59**

Name _____ Nancy's Help

Read the passage and answer the questions on the following page.

Nancy's Help

Nancy was up early on Saturday to help her father with an important job. They were going to paint the fence in the yard. Mr. Bickers, Nancy's father, had gotten all the supplies the day before. So, everything was all ready to go.

After breakfast, Nancy and her father went outside to begin their work. They carried out buckets of paint, brushes, and cloths. Nancy helped her father open the paint cans and place all of the supplies around the work area. Next, they opened the paint cans and began working. Nancy was impressed by how nice it looked when they spread the clean white paint over the dull gray wood. This was going to make their yard look beautiful in spring with the green grass, colorful flowers, and white fence.

The painters worked for several minutes when Nancy's mom came to tell her husband of a phone call. Mr. Bickers went inside to take the call and soon returned to tell Nancy that he would be gone a few minutes longer. He encouraged her to continue working and he would return shortly. Nancy nodded and kept painting. In fact she kept painting until she had completed the entire front yard side of the fence.

About thirty minutes later, Nancy's father returned. He was very surprised at her progress. Nancy had really done a lot of work! Mr. Bickers hugged his daughter and thanked her for doing such a great job. Nancy smiled and said it was okay because she had fun doing it. The rest of the afternoon the two partners worked on completing the project. Tired and splotched with paint drops, the pair finally finished their masterpiece at 4:00 p.m.

To admire their work, they decided to prepare glasses of fresh lemonade, sit on the porch, and watch the sun go down. That was really a day's work. Mr. Bickers and his number one painting partner had done an excellent job.

60 © Carson-Dellosa CD-2204

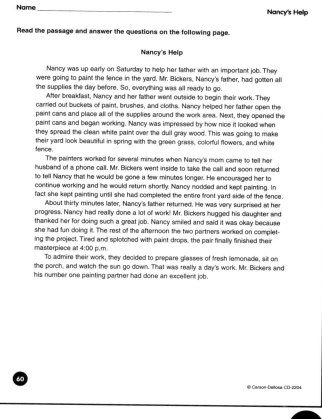

Name _____ Nancy's Help

Read each question. Circle the letter beside the correct answer.

1. What was Nancy going to help her father do?
   A. wash the dog
   B. paint the house
   (C) paint the fence
   D. make lemonade

2. Why did Nancy have to work alone for awhile?
   A. Her father wanted to see how much she could do by herself.
   B. Mrs. Bickers needed to see Nancy's father for a few minutes.
   (C) Mr. Bickers received a phone call.
   D. They ran out of supplies and her father went to get more.

3. How did Nancy's father react when he returned?
   (A) He was surprised that she had done so much work.
   B. He was disappointed that she was not all finished.
   C. He was tired and wanted to stop for the day.
   D. He was worried that it might start to rain.

4. What did Nancy and her father do to celebrate?
   A. They went out to dinner that evening with Nancy's mom.
   B. Nancy's dad bought her a surprise.
   (C) They sat on the porch with lemonade and looked at their work.
   D. They decided to become professional fence painters to make money.

5. What does the author mean by the use of the word "masterpiece"?
   A. Every time someone paints they create a masterpiece.
   (B) Painted works of art are sometimes called masterpieces.
   C. Working outside painting houses and fences is often called masterpiece work.
   D. Masterpieces are usually artistic paintings that are painted white like their fence.

Total Problems:	Total Correct:	Score:

61

© Carson-Dellosa CD-2204

Name _____ Catherine's Catch

Read the passage and the statements that follow. Decide if each statement is true or false. Place a T or F in the blank next to each statement.

Catherine's Catch

It was the first day of basketball season and Catherine was on the team! She had been looking forward to the chance to play on the all-girl team for two years. Finally, it was here and she was ready. Practices had started over two weeks ago and now it was time for the first game. She proudly dressed in her gold and white Eagles jersey and shorts to join her team at the school gymnasium.

Catherine was one of the first team members to arrive. She went to the locker room to put away her things. She soon found a few friends and began practicing drills with them. In a little while, the entire team was there and the coach was giving his pregame talk. He talked about how careful they needed to be in the game. The other team, the Pirates, is very good and it is hard to get the ball away from them. Coach Bryan told the team that a win was possible, as long as everyone would concentrate.

The horn sounded and the teams took the court. The first play of the game was a clear shot from center court to the net from the Pirates team. The shot would have been perfect, but the ball moved and the goal was missed. Lisa, Catherine's best friend, caught the ball, tossed it to Catherine for a lay up and two points were now on the board for the Eagles!

The Pirates took possession of the ball as well as the score board for the rest of the first half. Then, the Eagles came on to claim victory! Catherine was pleased with her team's performance. And she was especially pleased with her own. This was going to be a great season!

1. __T__ Catherine is on the Eagle's team.

2. __F__ The team had not practiced before the game.

3. __T__ The Pirates were a tough team to beat.

4. __F__ Most of the players on the teams were boys.

5. __F__ Coach Bryan was Catherine's father.

6. __T__ The first shot by the Eagles scored two points.

7. __F__ The Pirates won the game.

62

Total Problems:	Total Correct:	Score:

© Carson-Dellosa CD-2204

Name _____ Catherine's Catch

Refer to the passage on page 62 to solve this puzzle.

Catherine's Catch Crossword Puzzle

Across
2 the team Catherine's team played against
3 the period of months a sport is played
8 an area for players to store their things and change clothes (two words)
9 the opposite of lose
10 the Eagle's coach (his last name)

Down
1 the name of Catherine's team
4 the large (usually lighted) screen that displays the scores
5 the name of the uniform shirt
6 an enclosed area often used for indoor school sports
7 an organized group of players for a sport

Total Problems:	Total Correct:	Score:

63

© Carson-Dellosa CD-2204

Name _____ Natalia's Place

Read the passage and answer the questions on the following page.

Natalia's Place

"I need someone to take care of Natalia for a few weeks," she heard her father say. "Her mother is sick, and I need to take care of her as she recovers."

Natalia crept back into her bedroom. Early the next morning her father awakened her. "Natalia, Aunt Becca is here to take you home with her."

Natalia knew she would miss her parents and didn't want to go away and stay in a strange place, though she had visited there once before. She remembered Florence, her cousin. Florence was mature for her age, and said, "My name is Florence. Friends call me 'Flo' for short."

She was glad to see Florence's big smile and open arms. One day Florence said, "Come quickly, Natalia. I have something to show you."

The two girls raced across a field of wildflowers and into the woods. Down a steep bank they skidded and landed feet first beside a little brook. "Look Natalia," said Florence. "I made this myself." There in the stream was a water wheel made from branches and wooden blades. Each piece was fitted perfectly together and turned smoothly in the clear, cool stream.

"What does it do?" asked Natalia.

"Oh, it doesn't *do* anything. It is just to enjoy. I like to watch the water flow by, and listen to the wheel go 'slap, slap, slap' as it turns in the stream. It is peaceful, and reminds me that life is good, but that it takes a lot of cooperation to make it so. You know, the branches, the wooden paddles, the brook, and of course, my handiwork!" They both laughed. It was the first time Natalia had laughed since she had left home.

The girls visited the little brook whenever they had a chance to relax. Often Natalia would just lie on her back, watching the green leaves above, and listening to the slap, slap, slap of the little wheel in the brook. Whenever she missed her family, she would think that she was doing her part to help her mother by staying with Florence for a while.

When her mother got well and she returned home, Natalia told her mother of the little brook. "I called it Natalia's place," she said. "Whenever I felt lonely, I would go there and remember that life is good, but that it takes a lot of cooperation to make it so."

"Maybe one day you will take me to Natalia's place," her mother said, as she hugged and kissed her. "I'm glad you were with Florence while I was recovering."

64

© Carson-Dellosa CD-2204

Name _____   Natalia's Place

Read each question. Circle the letter beside the correct answer.

1. Why did Natalia have to go away?
    A. Her father had to work.
    (B) Her mother was sick.
    C. Her cousin was very lonely.
    D. She was on a vacation.

2. What did Natalia think about leaving home?
    (A) She didn't want to go because she would miss her parents.
    B. She was scared of airplanes.
    C. She was excited and begged to go.
    D. She was unhappy and refused to go.

3. What did Flo show her cousin?
    (A) a water wheel
    B. a tree house
    C. a trail in the woods
    D. her new doll house

4. When do Flo and Natalia visit the brook?
    A. when they are hiding from Flo's little brother
    (B) when they have a chance to relax
    C. when it is almost time to go eat supper
    D. when it is summer and they have free time

5. What could Florence mean by the phrase "it takes a lot of cooperation to make it so"?
    (A) People need each other during difficult times in life.
    B. The water wheel has different parts that work together.
    C. Florence needed help making the water wheel.
    D. Natalia should cooperate more with her mother.

© Carson-Dellosa CD-2204 | Total Problems: Total Correct: Score: | **65**

Name _____   Katia's Airplane Ride

Read the passage and answer the questions on the following page.

Katia's Airplane Ride

Katia's father is an airline pilot who flies all over the world. Sometimes he is gone for weeks at the time. One day when Katia came home from school her father said, "Katia, I have a surprise for you."

Katia was excited. "What is it?" she cried.

"It will have to wait until tomorrow," her father said.

The next day was Saturday. Katia was up at dawn. In the kitchen, her father had fixed a big breakfast. "We have to eat a big breakfast for our surprise today," he said.

Katia and her father drove out of town to a small airport. There were several small airplanes parked near the little hangar.

"Katia," her father said. "You have always wanted to ride in an airplane. I have an even better surprise. You will ride and you will also fly the airplane today. That is, if you want to."

"Do I want to?" Katia exclaimed. "That has always been my dream."

Katia walked quickly to a small blue and white, single engine airplane with her father. Her father explained each thing he did as they prepared to fly. Once in the air, Katia gazed out the window. "It is beautiful," she said. "I love it up here!"

"Now, Katia," said her father, "it is your turn to fly. Just do what I say, and you will be fine. These are dual controls, so I will be your backup at all times."

At first they just flew straight and level. Then, her father said, "How about a turn or two?"

"Let's do it!" Katia said.

Much too soon, Katia saw the airport come into view. "Do we have to land now?" she asked. "I'm afraid so," her father said. "We only have the airplane for one hour. But how about doing this again?"

"Do you have to ask?" Katia asked with a twinkle in her eye. "I can hardly wait."

"Well," her father said with a big grin, "I think I have a budding pilot on my hands."

66   © Carson-Dellosa CD-2204

Name _____   Katia's Airplane Ride

Read each question. Circle the letter beside the correct answer.

1. Why did Katia get up early the morning of the surprise?
    A. She was so excited about the airplane trip.
    (B) She wanted to find out what the surprise was.
    C. She wanted to help her mother make breakfast.
    D. She hoped her parents were getting her a pony.

2. Where did Katia's father take her?
    A. to the airport where he works
    (B) to a small airport out of town
    C. to an airplane museum
    D. to an amusement park with plane rides

3. What had always been Katia's dream?
    A. to ride in an airplane
    B. to pretend she was a bird
    C. to see a real airport
    (D) to fly an airplane

4. How long was Katia's airplane ride?
    A. two hours
    (B) one hour
    C. three hours
    D. four hours

5. How was Katia's father able to control the plane even while Katia was using her controls?
    A. The airplane just knew who was the real pilot.
    B. The airplane was not really controlled by Katia's controls.
    (C) The airplane had dual controls.
    D. The airplane was not going fast enough for the controls to work.

6. What did Katia say about doing this event another time?
    A. no
    B. maybe
    C. She was too scared to say.
    (D) yes

© Carson-Dellosa CD-2204 | Total Problems: Total Correct: Score: | **67**

Name _____   The Train

Read the passage and answer the questions on the following page.

The Train

Only four months ago my family moved to a new house. It is a nice house and has lots of space for our family of five, but it doesn't seem like home yet. Our old house was much closer to town and we lived near the railroad tracks. The train would come by almost every hour and blow its horn. My sister, Leigh, and I would stand in our backyard and wave to the conductor as the enormous engine passed us. Our new house is far from any railroads, streets, or other houses. My parents say they like the privacy of the new house, but I miss the excitement of the old place.

I remember when we first moved to the old house and the train would often scare me at night. But, in only a few weeks I was used to the horn and I began to anticipate the rhythmic clatter of the wheels on the tracks. It was home and I miss it now. So many days after school, I would lie in the grass in the backyard and stare at the clouds, thinking. Then I would feel the vibration of the train's approach and soon the horn would sound. I would sit up and scream at the top of my voice, only to be drowned out by the sound of the horn. I was amazed by the way the sounds were mixing together, and the stronger sound was the only one to be heard.

I guess those days are gone now and I will begin to discover new things that are unique about our new house. I will miss the old house and neighborhood. But, now that we are here, Leigh and I love playing in the giant backyard and running as fast as we can over the grassy hill in the corner of the yard. I think this place will become a favorite as well. The clouds are certainly easy to see out here. And I still love to lie on the grass and just think about things.

68   © Carson-Dellosa CD-2204

Panel 1 (page 69) — The Train

Name _____   The Train

Read each question and write your answer in the space provided.

1. What is the main idea of this story? The narrator has moved to a new house and misses the train that used to pass by the old house.

2. What does the narrator miss about the old house? the train

3. Why was the narrator amazed by the train's horn and its loudness? Because when he or she screams the train's horn is heard, not the scream.

4. Who enjoyed running on the grassy hill in the new house's yard? the narrator and his sister, Leigh

5. Where would the person telling the story do a lot of thinking? Lying on the grass watching the clouds in the sky.

© Carson-Dellosa CD-2204 | Total Problems: | Total Correct: | Score: | 69

Panel 2 (page 70) — Mr. Borg Visits Russia

Name _____   Mr. Borg Visits Russia

Read the passage and answer the questions on the following page.

Mr. Borg Visits Russia

In early spring, Mr. Borg visited St. Petersburg, Russia. As the airplane landed, he saw large patches of snow among the leafless birch trees. The airport had been cleared of snow, but the weather was still too cold for leaves and blossoms.

As the bus crossed the river, Mr. Borg saw an icebreaker ship opening the way for shipping traffic. He had never seen an icebreaker at work before. The bus stopped at a beautiful museum called "The Hermitage," built by Peter the Great, a Russian emperor.

As Mr. Borg toured the Hermitage, he saw a group of school children and a teacher on a field trip. Right away, the children recognized Mr. Borg's strange accent. They crowded around him chattering in Russian.

One of the girls spoke English. "Are you an American?" she asked. "Yes, I am," he said. "Oh, good. My name is Irina. My friends want me to ask you some questions. May I?" she asked. "Of course," he replied.

"What is your name?" Irina asked

"My name is Walter Borg," he said. Irina translated as Mr. Borg spoke.

"Where do you live?" she asked.

"I live in the United States of America, in a state called Georgia," he said.

"Do you have a dog?" Irina asked.

"Yes, I have two dogs. They are Brittany and Dolly."

When Irina translated, a boy asked, "How big are they?"

"They are this big," Mr Borg said, holding his hands about ten inches apart.

The teacher hurried over and spoke some excited words in Russian.

"What did she say?" Mr. Borg asked.

"We have to hurry now. We are late for the next tour," Irina said. "May we have your autograph?"

Mr. Borg signed autographs as the children crowded around. The teacher led the children on through the Hermitage. Irina turned back and said, "Thank you for talking with us. You gave me a chance to practice my English."

70   © Carson-Dellosa CD-2204

Panel 3 (page 71) — Mr. Borg Visits Russia

Name _____   Mr. Borg Visits Russia

Read each question. Circle the letter beside the correct answer.

1. What kind of weather does Russia have in Spring?
   A. hot
   B. snowy
   C. rainy
   D. dry

2. With whom did Mr. Borg talk at the museum?
   A. an American
   B. Irina
   C. a teacher
   D. a tour guide

3. Who was Peter the Great?
   A. He was a great writer in Russia.
   B. He was the president of Russia.
   C. He was a famous emperor of Russia.
   D. He worked at the museum.

4. Why did Mr. Borg tell about his dogs?
   A. The children asked him about them.
   B. People saw them while he was walking.
   C. His dogs looked like the ones in the paintings.
   D. He didn't talk about his dogs.

5. Why did Irina's teacher hurry the children along?
   A. Because they were going to be late for the movie.
   B. Because they were leaving the museum and the buses were leaving.
   C. Because their tour was about to begin.
   D. Because they were not eating their lunches fast enough.

6. How did Mr. Borg travel to Russia for his visit?
   A. car   **B. airplane**
   C. boat   D. train

7. For what did Irina thank Mr. Borg before she left?
   A. She thanked him for talking to her so she could practice her English.
   B. She thanked him for giving her some candy.
   C. She thanked him for helping her find her teacher.
   D. She thanked him for sharing his lunch with her.

© Carson-Dellosa CD-2204 | Total Problems: | Total Correct: | Score: | 71

Panel 4 (page 72) — Mr. Borg Visits Russia Crossword Puzzle

Name _____   Mr. Borg Visits Russia

Refer to the passage on page 70 to solve this puzzle.

Mr. Borg Visits Russia Crossword Puzzle

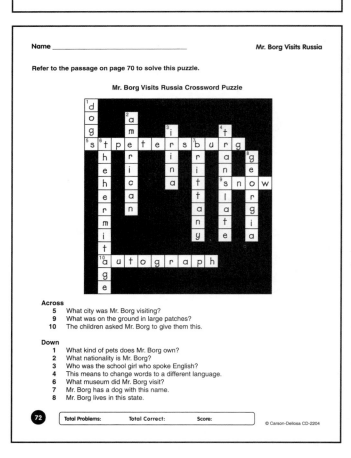

Across
5. What city was Mr. Borg visiting?
9. What was on the ground in large patches?
10. The children asked Mr. Borg to give them this.

Down
1. What kind of pets does Mr. Borg own?
2. What nationality is Mr. Borg?
3. Who was the school girl who spoke English?
4. This means to change words to a different language.
6. What museum did Mr. Borg visit?
7. Mr. Borg has a dog with this name.
8. Mr. Borg lives in this state.

72 | Total Problems: | Total Correct: | Score: | © Carson-Dellosa CD-2204

Name _____ A Camping Trip

Read the passage and answer the questions on the following page.

A Camping Trip

Juan and his brother Mark wanted to go camping. Their mother, Mrs. Gomez, said, "I'll take you if your school work is completed and done well."

"Oh, great!" they said in one voice.

"We'll work hard. We promise!" Juan said.

Finally the day came for the camping trip. Each day after school, Mrs. Gomez had taken the boys to a store to get items on the checklist she had helped them to prepare: food, water, repair kits for camp gear, fuel for the camp stove, more food, everything they would need for a weekend in the woods.

Friday afternoon, in a heavy rain, Mrs. Gomez and the boys loaded their gear and headed for the national park. Long before dark, the rain stopped and they set up camp and started a campfire. Mrs. Gomez had prepared "bucket stew" at home. When the fire was ablaze, she hung the stew pot over the flames and soon the wonderful aroma of "bucket stew" filled the campsite.

Early the next morning, Mrs. Gomez went to the dock to fish. The boys wanted to fix "fire toast." The first two slices of bread burned badly. Soon they learned to make crisp, brown "fire toast," covered in blackberry jam given to them by Grandmother Gomez.

There were plenty of fish for supper, for everyone had caught lots of fish that day. Mrs. Gomez even caught a large trout. "I'll prepare this one tonight and put it in the cooler. For breakfast tomorrow, it will be a real treat."

Soon, it was time to break camp and pack for home. Mrs. Gomez taught the boys how to clean their equipment and pack it for use the next time. Juan said, "I will be very careful with this equipment, because I want to be ready to go camping again soon." Mark said, "I have already started making a new checklist. I learned a lot on this trip."

As Mrs. Gomez drove home, both boys peppered her with questions about their next camping trip. "A couple more trips like this," she said, "and we'll be ready for a camping vacation in the mountains, or a canoe trip in Canada."

"All right!!" Mark said.

"Yes!" exclaimed Juan.

Name _____ A Camping Trip

Read each question. Circle the letter beside the correct answer.

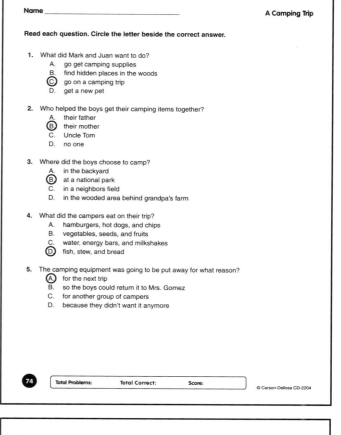

1. What did Mark and Juan want to do?
   A. go get camping supplies
   B. find hidden places in the woods
   C. go on a camping trip
   D. get a new pet

2. Who helped the boys get their camping items together?
   A. their father
   B. their mother
   C. Uncle Tom
   D. no one

3. Where did the boys choose to camp?
   A. in the backyard
   B. at a national park
   C. in a neighbors field
   D. in the wooded area behind grandpa's farm

4. What did the campers eat on their trip?
   A. hamburgers, hot dogs, and chips
   B. vegetables, seeds, and fruits
   C. water, energy bars, and milkshakes
   D. fish, stew, and bread

5. The camping equipment was going to be put away for what reason?
   A. for the next trip
   B. so the boys could return it to Mrs. Gomez
   C. for another group of campers
   D. because they didn't want it anymore

| Total Problems: | Total Correct: | Score: |

Name _____ A Camping Trip

Refer to the passage on page 73 to solve this puzzle.

A Camping Trip Crossword Puzzle

Across

1 a source of heat for a campsite
3 where Mrs. Gomez went to fish
7 sweet stuff Grandmother Gomez made (two words)
8 needed to make the camp stove work

Down

2 the day after Thursday
4 a list that helps you pack necessary items for a trip
5 Mark's brother
6 type of fish Mrs. Gomez caught and cooked for breakfast
7 The boys burned this while making "fire toast."

| Total Problems: | Total Correct: | Score: |

Name _____ The Monkey Bars At Last

Read the passage and answer the questions on the following page.

The Monkey Bars at Last!

Every Wednesday our physical education class doesn't go to the gym. Instead, we go to the playground for a physical fitness test. We all have to participate in order to earn free time afterwards, but the whole test is pretty fun. We start on the first set of equipment at the back of the playground and follow a path to each of the other activities. At the end we get our elapsed time from the coach's stopwatch.

I like the fitness course and I like to see if I can make it through the entire course faster each time I do it. Coach Warner says we are his best class for this activity. We begin with the long jump, then go to this wall we have to climb over, then swing across a puddle of water. The last few challenges are to jump in and out of tires lying on the ground, run diagonally back and forth through wooden pegs, and finally hit the monkey bars to swing into the finish line! It is a lot of fun to get to the monkey bars because you know you're finished at that point.

My best friend, Kathy, likes this fitness course, too. Ken, a boy in our class, is always trying to beat us and get a better time than ours. He has only beaten my time once, and that was because I lost my shoe as I was climbing over the wall. Kathy is very fast and Ken has never beaten her. I think that is great. She is a fast runner and her only competitor in running is Lee, another boy in our school. He is very fast, also.

We have only a few more Wednesdays left this year to do the fitness test, so we have to do our best each time. We certainly don't want anyone to break our records! Maybe next year we can get even better at it.

Name _____   The Monkey Bars At Last

Read each statement. Decide if it is true or false. Place a T or F in the blank next to each statement.

1. __F__ Ken is a faster runner than Kathy.

2. __T__ The monkey bars are the last item on the fitness test.

3. __T__ One challenge on the fitness test is to swing over a puddle of water.

4. __T__ Coach Warner is the physical education teacher.

5. __F__ The fitness tests are done on Tuesdays.

6. __F__ Lee is not a very fast runner.

Read each question. Circle the letter beside the correct answer.

7. How many challenges are in the fitness test?
   A. 5
   B. 6
   C. 7
   D. 4

8. Where is the fitness test equipment located?
   A. on the front of the playground
   B. at the back of the playground
   C. in the gymnasium
   D. not given

9. Who is telling the story?
   A. Kenny
   B. Lee
   C. Kathy's friend
   D. Coach Warner

10. How do the students know how fast they complete the test?
   A. The coach times them on his stopwatch.
   B. The students time each other.
   C. The students estimate the time mentally.
   D. There is a clock in the gym that tells the time.

© Carson-Dellosa CD-2204

| Total Problems: | Total Correct: | Score: |

77

Name _____   The Monkey Bars at Last

Refer to the passage on page 76 to solve this puzzle.

The Monkey Bars at Last Crossword Puzzle

Across

2 The narrator lost hers once climbing over the wall.

3 a common name for a leader of a sports team or physical education teacher

4 to get better with practice

6 the last item on the fitness test (two words)

Down

1 One event requires the runners to jump in and out of these.

2 a device used for timing things very precisely

3 The runners have to _____ over this wall in the test.

5 the boy in the school who can run the fastest

78

| Total Problems: | Total Correct: | Score: |

© Carson-Dellosa CD-2204